Given to
McKenzie Do
at NHS ind.
ceremony. (Sophor

# Unwrap Your Gift

## Discover and Become
## All You Were Born to Be!

### Henry A. Penix

Tulsa, Oklahoma

UNWRAP YOUR GIFT
© 2005 by Henry A. Penix

Published by Insight Publishing Group
8801 S. Yale, Suite 410
Tulsa, OK 74137
918-493-1718

Illustrations by: Brannon Carnes
B.C. Studios
P.O. Box 9527
Michigan City, IN 46361

ISBN 1-932503-41-2
1. Business  2. Self-help  3. Psychology  4. Christian Living

Library of Congress catalog card number: 2004113272

Printed in the United States of America

# ℘ *Dedication* ℘

I would like to dedicate this book to those of you who will begin to discover your unique talents, realize your full potential, and become ALL you were born to be as we unwrap your gift together!

# *Endorsements*

"Henry A. Penix has done an outstanding job of outlining the steps for you to become all you were created to be. This book truly is a gift for your life. Read it!"

**—Ken Blanchard**
**Co-author**
**The One Minute Manager**

"Of all the success stories I've heard, I can only think of a few that carry the impact that Henry A. Penix's does. Hearing about the journey that Henry and his wife made to get where they are today, a place of true success, really touched me personally...a tremendous testimony that needs to be heard."

**—Peter Lowe**
**President of *Get Motivated* Success Seminars**

"Your program has given me the tools necessary to balance my life. Now my priorities and finances are in line, and I even have time to do things for myself."

**—Tulsa Real Estate Agent**

"Using the principles in your program I started my own company and doubled my income thanks to your explosive message and the powerful step-by-step system."

**—New York City Businessman**

"I'm thankful that your program covers all aspects of my life! I have a much better understanding of my life's purpose and passion. I've made crucial changes heading in a new, more fulfilling and successful direction."

**—Las Vegas Salesman**

# *Contents*

Acknowledgments
Foreword
Introduction

# Acknowledgments

I would like to acknowledge the following people:

**My wife** – Laurie, your love and support extends beyond my greatest expectations!

**My children** – Zac, Olivia, and Madison, you make life worth living! You'll understand more when you have children.

**Henry and Jewell** – My parent's who love and support me unconditionally. I'm forever grateful for my upbringing.

**Paul & Jane Meyer** – My mentors who inspire me to always do more for others.

**Michelle & Heather** – For contributing the "missing links."

**The staff at HAPM & AYD** – For their dedication and hard work in making dreams come true.

**Brian Mast of Pilot Communications Group** – A great writer/editor with a heart of gold.

**John Mason of Insight Publishing** – A man of many talents who knows how to get the job done well.

To everyone whose name I didn't mention but were very significant in helping me complete this book. You know who you are—Thank you!

# *Foreword*

ℬ                                                    ℭ

## By Paul J. Meyer

Are you ready for something more meaningful? Something more exciting? Something that interests you and energizes you? Then congratulations—you have selected the right book to read!

*Unwrap Your Gift: Discover & Become ALL You Were Born to Be* will help you to use more of your God-given talents and abilities and help you find more fulfillment in life than you ever thought possible.

Henry A. Penix is a unique person well qualified to write this book, for he practices the principles and steps to success he presents. Not only is the content based on valid principles, but the author delivers his message in a reader-friendly style, structured logically so that one principle builds upon another.

You will find this book intriguing because it focuses on what is possible when people discover who they really are and the special significance for which they were born. You will find this book interesting because it provides numerous and varied examples of the exceptional people from all walks of life who have successfully made this discovery.

Positive expectancy pervades *Unwrap Your Gift: Discover & Become ALL You Were Born to Be.* This is an attitude and approach to life I have studied, practiced, and advocated for decades. Henry's effectiveness reflects his ability to transform this essential attitude into action, and his book demonstrates his ability to persuade others to do likewise.

As Henry says, "Everyone is born for special significance in life," but too few people achieve it. Refuse to let this happen to you! Begin the exciting journey down the path of introspection to discover who you are. Learn from the success stories in this book. Learn also from the precarious pitfalls of others the author points out.

I appreciate Henry A. Penix for providing this important book, and I commend you for reading it and extend to you my best wishes for your personal achievement and fulfillment as you read and carry out the life-changing message in *Unwrap Your Gift: Discover & Become ALL You Were Born to Be.*


Paul J. Meyer
Founder of Success Motivation© International, Inc.
And 40+ other companies
*New York Times* Best-Selling Author
Latest book: *Unlock Your Legacy: 25 Keys for Success*

Everyone is born for special significance in life but very few people ever find it and yet fewer actually achieve it! *Unwrap Your Gift* will lead you down the path of introspection to discover who you really are and the special significance you were born for.

Yesterday was your past, tomorrow is your future, and today is your gift—that is why it is called your present!

Your talents, potential, and significance are all part of your unique gift—that thing that lives on the inside of each of us that is rarely used to its fullest. *Unwrap Your Gift* will help you discover untapped potential and talents that you didn't even know you had, then show you how to use them—all of them!

Follow me to a place where dreams really do come true. Let's unwrap your gift together and celebrate the unveiling of your unique significance!

Then let's discover how to take the steps necessary to tap into your full potential, realize your dreams, and become ALL that you were born to be.

In the inspiring words of Nelson Mandela:

> Our deepest fear is not that we are inadequate. Our deepest fear is that we are powerful beyond all measure. It is our light not our darkness that

most frightens us. We ask ourselves who am I to be brilliant or gorgeous or talented or even fabulous? Actually who are we not to be? You are a child of the universe. Your playing small does not serve the world. There is nothing so enlightening about shrinking so that other people won't feel insecure around you. We are born to make manifest the glory of God, which is in each of us. It is not just in some of us, but it is in all of us. And as we let our own light shine, we unconsciously give other people permission to do the same. As we are liberated from our own fears, our presence automatically liberates others.

# Chapter One

# Born for Significance
# —Treasures Within

*Y*ou have a special gift, wrapped in a package. You have had this package for a while now, *but have you ever wondered what was inside?*

Each time you say to yourself, "What more could there be to life?" or "I'm really not happy with everything in my life right now" or "I'm ready for a change," the contents of your package begin to come more into focus.

In this package sits your unique gift! Wondering what it is? Excited? Apprehensive? Enthused? Want to tear into it like a kid at Christmas? Let's take our time and open it in such a way that will help and not frustrate you.

If I turned my children loose in a candy store, without instruction or guidelines, they would probably leave with a very sick and upset stomach. However, if they pace themselves and understand certain guidelines, they will have the time of their lives!

Your gift has been sitting here for quite some time. Some say even before you were born your gift was prepared just for your enjoyment. Others say your gift arrives when you go looking for it. Either way, when I found my gift, my life changed forever!

Before I discovered my gift:

I couldn't even afford $130 worth of wedding rings. I had to put them on a twelve-month charge that took three times to get approved!

- ❏ My relationships were all but nonexistent.

- ❏ My health was in question.

- ❏ Everything I tried to do failed.

- ❏ I began to wonder why I was even born.

Now, it is the exact opposite! Financial independence, a loving family, great health, fantastic relationships, and a sense of purpose—the difference is astounding! I love my life and I love who I've become!

I am a very "to the point" type of person and have meticulously reviewed every word written within this book many times. I say that so when you are reading you will take your time and absorb each word, sentence, paragraph, and page to its fullest. Each word was written for a specific reason and in a specific order. When your gift is revealed and you have learned how to implement it into your everyday life, separating yourself from the other 99 percent of the population, you'll be so glad you took the time!

Questions will be asked of you that will provoke thought, so please have a special journal or notebook ready to record them. At a later time you will be able to review and meditate on your newfound revelations.

Lastly, please note that everything learned from each chapter will be used in subsequent chapters, so please read the chapters in order. At the end of each chapter there are questions and exercises that are essential to your success. Please complete each so that you too may become ALL you were born to be!

Ready?

Let's get started!

## You were born for significance

Everyone in life is born for significance. You were too! It doesn't matter if you arrived in life as the result of an unplanned birth, a violent act of rape, a single parent birth, or from loving parents. *YOU are here for a reason and your life DOES have significance!*

Do not think for a minute that you are here by accident or that your life has no meaning. There are stories of countless people who were born destined for a seemingly destructive life without hope, without help, and without direction.

Yet these people grew beyond their circumstances and environment into ALL they were born to be. No matter what the odds were against them or no matter who said they would never make it, they succeeded. Some even succeeded on a very large scale.

## Dave Pelzer

Dave Pelzer was able to survive a horrific childhood and turn his experience into something positive. He now helps others learn how to move past their history and live a more fulfilling life. His most recent book, *Help Yourself*, has been nominated for the Pulitzer Prize. In it, he writes about how to survive and overcome difficult situations.

Pelzer was born to a firefighter and homemaker in the middle-class suburbs of San Francisco in 1960. For four years, his life was almost normal, but then his alcoholic mother began to ritualistically torture and abuse Dave. His mother cared for the rest of the children in the family, but starved, beat, and burned Dave regularly. He was first referred to as, "The boy," and eventually, "It." Dave internalized his mother's hatred and believed he was unworthy of love.

No one stepped in to stop Dave's mother, not even his passive father. Everyone just ignored "It."

His survival came down to a battle of outwitting his mother. Public school was his only protection. He found a haven there, stealing extra food from the cafeteria to stay alive. Two of Dave's fifth grade teachers eventually risked their careers to stop the ongoing violence in his family.

He remembers vividly the day when a police officer came to his school and told him, "I'm here to protect and serve you. You are free!"

Dave thought he was going to a prison, so he requested clean sheets and a hamburger! The police officer repeated, "No, son, you're free!" That's when everything clicked and Dave realized he was not ever going back to his mother.

Dave Pelzer had to break free from a lifetime of anguish that many will never face. He could have easily succumbed to it, but he faced it head-on with courage, persistence, and determination.

Today, he is the author of two prize-winning books and has dedicated his life to helping others. "I don't think I'd change one moment in my life," he explains, "because that would take away from my gratitude, from being humble."

What an attitude!

## Mawi Asgedom

In the African state of Ethiopia in 1973, a baby was born to a poor, overwhelmed family. Mawi Asgedom and his family endured the typical hardships of Ethiopian life: lack of proper food and water while war and famine plagued the land.

After spending years in a refugee camp and trekking through the brutal deserts of Africa, Mawi and his family escaped to the United States with no money, but hearts full of dreams

Poor didn't even begin to describe their lives. His first birthday party ever occurred on his twelfth birthday; he didn't even know what a birthday cake was, let alone birthday gifts. When his mother went to the grocery store, she returned to say that the pet food aisle contained more food than most Ethiopians would see in their lifetimes.

Mawi didn't speak or read any English, he was frail and out of place, and he didn't know any of the customs we take for granted. As a result, he was the brunt of other children's mean jokes and ridicule.

But Mawi was not one to give up. He had walked through the deserts of Africa at age eight behind his mother ... the skin completely peeled off of her feet. "If she can keep walking, so can I," he had said to himself. That became his mantra as he faced the new challenges ahead of him.

Mawi has taken full advantage of what America has to offer. His parents told him that school was the way to do well in America and he listened. "You just don't give up—that's the key," he says. He received a scholarship to Harvard and was chosen by his class to give the commencement speech at graduation.

Mawi has since attended law school and written a book entitled, *Of Beetles and Angels.* Mawi's father had advised him: "Treat all people, even the most unsightly beetles, as though they were angels from heaven." The results of those words and unbelievable courage in the face of impossible odds have brought Mawi to his unimagined success in life.

## Joni Eareckson Tada

Joni Eareckson Tada was once an accomplished swimmer. Today, she is a quadriplegic due to a tragic diving accident. She spends her time painting, writing, and traveling the world. She challenges people across the globe to consider their strengths, not their weaknesses.

## Barbara Walters

Barbara Walters had a lisp, yet by studying word pronunciation and working hard, she has become one of the best-known broadcast journalists of our time.

## Franklin Delano Roosevelt

Franklin Delano Roosevelt had polio when he became president of the United States.

## Beethoven

Beethoven was deaf when he composed his 9th Symphony.

## Become ALL you were really born to be

These are just a few of literally millions of untold stories. Each person overcame significant odds and adversity to ultimately become ALL they were born to be. You can do the same!

They never would have made it if they had let the "feeling sorry for myself" mentality override their desire to succeed.

I realize that everyone at some time or another has contemplated giving up. The cemeteries are full of people with unrealized potential; people who said, "If only I would have" or "I really should have."

Fortunately, because you are still breathing and reading this book now, it is not too late!

Just as the earth is designed to spin at an exact speed without spinning into the abyss, so are you, equipped with just what you need, when you need it, with the inherent ability to move through life at just the right speed.

Just as the earth is positioned exactly far enough away from the sun so that we do not burn up, so are you, positioned in life exactly where you need to be to reach your maximum potential.

Even the rough times or hard places you may have found yourself in will ultimately act as stepping-stones to your future significance. Believe it or not, everything that has happened up until this point in your life has been for a reason. Remember all the success stories?

Just as birds were born to fly and fish were born to swim, so you were born for a purpose—**on purpose**.

I get so disgusted when I see people trying to become someone else or trying to live their lives to fulfill someone else's expectations of them. My friend John Mason wrote a great book entitled, *You Were Born An Original, Don't Die A Copy.* How true.

**If we are born for a purpose and on purpose, then why do so many fall short or just quit?**

# ᔕ NOW IT IS YOUR TURN ᘓ

Now it is time for you to think about your life's purpose. Grab a pen and paper and write "My Life's Purpose" across the top of the page. Without thinking too deeply, jot down everything that comes to your mind that might relate to why you think you're here on earth.

At this point, don't even worry about making sense or whether or not it is grammatically correct. In fact, go a little wild and write down anything you've ever wanted to do in life! This is for your eyes only—think BIG. Here are a few questions to consider:

1. **What do you enjoy doing?** (i.e., career, hobbies, pastimes, organizations you belong to, volunteer work, et cetera)

2. **What roles do you serve?** (i.e., spouse, parent, child, employee, student, Sunday school teacher, vice president of your child's PTA, soccer coach, et cetera)

3. **How would you describe your character?** (i.e., honest, strong work ethic, loyal, passionate, kind, gracious, et cetera)

4. **How would others describe you and your character?**

5. **What are you passionate about?** (i.e., career expansion, raising your children, volunteering at the homeless shelter, teaching the children at your church, et cetera)

**6. What would you do if money were no object?** If you had one billion dollars in your checking account—what would you do with your time?

If you can only write down a few words or sentences, don't worry. We will continue to expand on your ideas throughout the remainder of this book. Writing your dreams, goals, and desires on a piece of paper will serve as the basis for the rest of this book.

Please do not read any further until you've completed this step.

Now the exciting part—guess what? If you completed this exercise, you have not only **just taken the bow off your package**, but you have also separated yourself from the majority of the population who do not follow through with most things and therefore do not obtain their dreams, goals, or desires.

Believe it or not you have also just taken the first step towards **living in the top 1 percent of the population!**

# Chapter Two

# *The Path Least Traveled —Why Some May Stop*

*A*ccording to people I've spoken with from all around the world, it seems the primary reasons some of them give up and fall short of maximizing their full potential are as follows:

1. **They lack the self-confidence.** They may have had childhood experiences of parents, siblings, or friends telling them that they are a failure or constantly shooting down their ideas. If left unquestioned, this generally preconditions them for failure or even worse, they won't try at all.

2. **They try to live up to the expectations of others.** As a result, they never make decisions on their own, for their own good, or relevant to their own dreams, goals, or desires. These people are usually classified as "people pleasers."

3. **They are too afraid**. They won't even begin taking the steps necessary to do what is in their hearts, even for reasons that defy rational explanation. Fear, either real or imagined, stops many.

4. **They have been raised with a negative belief system**. Most likely, they never questioned their negative belief system; blindly accepting failure.

5. **They think it is impossible.** They don't believe they have the right connections, enough money, or raw talent needed for true success or for the realization of their individual significance. They may just give up and take what life throws at them.

Let's look at each area in more detail:

## #1—Lack of self-confidence

People without self-confidence have probably been told all their lives that they would fail and could never become better. As they accepted what others said about them as fact, a negative self-image developed. Because of a negative self-image, they will usually try something once or twice, only to give up, reinforcing their negative beliefs.

They may have been raised with dominating parents or a dominating sibling who made decisions for them, thus never allowing them to make their own decisions. Since they never made their own decisions they never developed skills to

> *"The difference between history's boldest accomplishments and its most staggering failures is often, simply, the diligent will to persevere."*
> —*Abraham Lincoln*

recover from mistakes that would have ultimately helped build the self-confidence needed for future success.

Or, they may have never received any type of support from family, friends, or co-workers and have all but given up as a failure!

**This person needs to realize that failure is an event and not a person.** You may fail at something several times, but that does not mean that you are a failure.

Do you remember how many times Thomas Edison tried to invent electricity and failed?

He failed over ten thousand times, but he never gave up. Edison later stated, "I have not failed. I've just found ten thousand ways that won't work!"

Can you guess who the man is in the following illustration by his list of failures?

> He failed in business in 1831. He was defeated for state legislator in 1832. He tried another business in 1833. It failed. His fiancé died in 1835. He had a nervous breakdown in 1836. In 1843 he ran for Congress and was defeated. He tried again in 1848 and was defeated again. He tried running for the Senate in 1855 and lost. The next year he ran for vice president and lost. In 1859 he ran for the Senate again and was defeated. In 1860, Abraham Lincoln was elected the sixteenth president of the United States!

"The difference between history's boldest accomplishments and its most staggering failures is often, simply, the diligent will to persevere," said Lincoln.

If your current circle of friends do not support your vision or help give you the confidence needed to continue, you may want to look for a new group of friends. Sometimes, you may even need to encourage yourself. Keep moving forward, don't give up and continue until your dreams, goals, and desires materialize!

On top of it all, society has preconditioned us with a microwave mentality that states:

☐ If I can't have it now, then I want something else.

☐ If it takes too much effort, then it must not be for me.

☐ If I have to wait until tomorrow, then I don't want it.

How ridiculous!

### *Asian Bamboo*

Consider the example of persistence by the Asian Bamboo species. After five years of watering, weeding, and fertilizing, the plant is barely visible. Then in a span of about six weeks it grows two and a half feet a day to ninety feet and higher. It grows so fast that you can literally hear it growing!

The question to ask is did the bamboo grow ninety feet in six weeks or did it grow ninety feet in five years? Obviously, it grew ninety feet in five years, for all the time when growth wasn't visible it was developing a massive root system that would later support its magnificent growth.

Can you see how the current circumstances in your life are developing your massive root system? Even if you don't see immediate results, know that you are developing a root system that will ultimately sustain and support your magnificent growth.

Keep the faith and continue pressing forward, continue to allow your roots to grow as deep as you will be tall and know that you will succeed.

## #2—Living up to other's expectations

People miss their true significance all the time by trying to live up to other people's expectations. These people are generally labeled "people pleasers" or "co-dependant" and seldom make decisions on their own, for their own good, or relevant to their own dreams, goals, and desires. They are really never sure about what they want themselves because they have spent all their time making sure everyone else is happy and receiving what they want!

Often, these "people pleasers" were ignored by their parents as children and therefore always sought to please others. Some grew up in abusive households, trying to maintain peace at the expense of their own dreams, goals, and desires.

A "people pleaser" can sometimes be confused with someone who is a "peacemaker" or has a "servant's heart." There is balance in the personality of a peacemaker and those with a servant's heart. I truly believe you can dedicate your life to serving others and still achieve your own dreams and realize your individual significance and potential.

If you have spent considerable time and energy trying to live up to the expectations of others or trying only to please everyone else, it is time for you to turn your focus back towards yourself.

Ask yourself:

❐ What motivates me?

❐ What are my interests?

❐ What makes me happy?

❐ If nobody cared, what would I do for an occupation?

❐ What would I do for a hobby?

❐ What have I always wanted to do—for me?

Stop and give these questions some thought, particularly if you are a "people pleaser," then write down your answers now.

When you finish, make a plan to incorporate those answers into your everyday life. You will find that the people around you will support you more than you ever imagined!

Think of ways you can slowly work towards what YOU really want to do in life, something that would make YOU happy and give YOU significance. As YOU begin to include some of these things for YOU, YOU will be much happier, more fulfilled, and able to relate to and help others more effectively.

Unfortunately, I have even seen others take advantage of "people pleasers" by playing circumstances or situations to their favor. It grieves me to see a husband recognize this trait in his wife and then take advantage of, or capitalize on the situation for his own benefit. Sometimes making his wife feel bad if he feels things aren't done just right, by his standards, thereby using her weakness for his own benefit. If the children pick up on this trait in their mom, sometimes the same games will be repeated. Once open communication is established and the family becomes aware of the problem, things will begin to change.

If you are a "people pleaser" and it's difficult for you to make others aware of the problem, find a support group to help, or talk to someone else who is a strong communicator and ask them to help coach you through communicating your feelings to others. Another option may be to put your feelings in writing and give them to the people you've been pleasing.

Most of the time it will be up to the "people pleaser" to recognize their condition and begin to talk to the people he or she has been "pleasing."

**If you have a servant's heart**, recognize that many of the most significant individuals in history who accomplished great feats were also servant hearted! Mother Teresa is a prime example. People supported

HER cause and allowed HER dreams to become true, thus making HER significance to society very apparent. Even though SHE dedicated HER life to serving others, SHE still achieved HER goals and lived a very fulfilled life.

If Mother Teresa had been someone who always tried to just please others—a "people pleaser," I'm sure her decisions to go into foreign countries would have been extinguished by others vying for her attention. SHE had a plan, SHE had goals, and SHE had significance throughout HER life as a servant even as she "pleased" millions! There is balance.

Please note that if a "people pleaser" changes overnight, fireworks are sure to ensue. However, if slow but sure steps are taken by first becoming aware that this condition exists and then making others aware, change will be welcomed.

Ultimately, changing from an overt "people pleaser" with no goals to a more balanced servant leader with personal aspirations will result in a much happier, healthier individual who will benefit society, others, and themselves much more!

## #3—Being full of fear

For those whose lack of progress is consistently blocked by fear, remember the following acronym for FEAR:

>  False
>  Evidence
>  Appearing
>  Real

Usually, fear is nothing but false evidence. Our imaginations spin out of control and we think the worst. We think it is real, and suddenly we are frozen! Right now, visualize yourself standing up and reaching out in front of you. Grab the hand of your future and allow it to pull you forward—toward your future.

Simultaneously, try to visualize reaching back and grabbing the hand of fear that always pulls you away from your future. This could be fear of using your abilities, fear of taking steps necessary to live your dreams, fear of what others may think of you, fear of success, fear of failure, et cetera.

Reaching forward and reaching backward, being pulled in two opposite directions at the same time doesn't work, does it?

You must let go of one or you will be ripped apart!

**Whichever YOU decide to agree with,** faith for the future or fear that is holding you back, **will be the one that determines the rest of your life.**

The choice is yours:

> **FAITH:** If you truly agree with your future and have faith in your future, then you will naturally let go of fear and begin moving forward toward your dreams, goals, and desires.

> **FEAR:** If you agree with your fears, then you will naturally let go of your future and remain stuck in your present, which immediately

becomes your past since the world around you is always moving forward.

Keep in mind that if you allow yourself to be pulled back towards fear, you alone are the one responsible for making that decision that will affect the rest of your life!

When you let go of fear and move forward with faith towards your future, wonderful things begin to happen. Fear, worry, and anxiety have a tendency to drain your energies. **Letting go of them will enable you to operate at maximum efficiency towards a bright future!**

## #4—Negative belief systems

Some people allow, usually unintentionally, their negative belief systems to hold them back from reaching their full potential.

A negative belief system is based on what is perceived to be factual information. If you are operating your life based on a negative belief system, it's generally not your fault. You have been given certain information that to the best of your knowledge was received and accepted as truth. Left unexamined or unquestioned, these "truths" develop into habits that could lead to limiting and even destructive behavior.

Have you ever been told:

☐ "You won't amount to much."

❏ "You'll never make it."

❏ "You are destined to fail."

❏ "Go back home where you belong."

❏ "You are a failure waiting to happen."

❏ "You're a loser."

Unfortunately, if your parents or any other significant person in your life (i.e., sibling, spouse, classmate, colleague, or friend) continually minimized you with negative statements like these—it will have an effect on your life. Psychologists have proven that whenever you hear something long enough, you internalize it and it becomes real to you, no matter if you believe it or not!

> *A negative belief system will not and cannot support your dreams, goals, or desires.*

I've spoken with hundreds of people who grew up with a negative belief system based solely on the opinion or comments of others. Complete lies, but after being internalized, they are accepted as "truths"! Later in life, they show up as various conditioned behaviors and in nearly all decision-making processes.

Others develop a negative belief system based on a series of life experiences. People have tried to justify and support their negative outlook by telling me:

❏ "I've been married three times—there's no hope,"

☐ "I've tried to start five businesses and failed,"

☐ "I don't have any friends,"

☐ "I'm sick all the time,"

☐ "Everything I try to do fails, so I must be a failure."

**Please understand—failing is an event, NOT a person.**
So many people in history have been called failures
and were given great opportunities to develop a
negative belief system . . . **but didn't.** Most of these
people went on to experience tremendous success.

### Jackie Robinson

Born the grandson of a slave on January 31, 1919 in the
Deep South, Jackie Robinson was the youngest of five
children. His father deserted him when Jackie was just
six months old, so Jackie's mother moved the family to
California. She hoped for a better life with less
segregation.

Young Jackie showed great promise. In 1941 he left
college, having used up his athletic eligibility, and
joined the Honolulu Bear's professional football team.
He was drafted into the United States Army in 1942
and for three years he and champion boxer Joe Louis tried
to eradicate the unfair treatment of minorities in the
military. Robinson was medically discharged in 1945.

He took bold steps into the world of baseball, joining the
Kansas City Monarchs Negro League in 1945 for four
hundred dollars per month. Robinson had no intention of

making baseball a career, but he shot to the top of the Monarch's League and grabbed the attention of Branch Rickey, innovative president of the Brooklyn Dodgers. Rickey was searching for the first black player for the major leagues, which was closed to minorities at that time.

When he signed with the Montreal Royals in 1945, a Dodger's farm team, the owners and sportswriters protested his integration, claiming it would destroy major league baseball. Rickey and Robinson remained confident—although because of segregation laws, Robinson was forced to ride in the back of buses. Sadly, games were even cancelled due to his presence. Players on the team circulated a petition demanding to play without Robinson. Adversity was the name of the game, not baseball.

In 1947, Robinson joined the Dodgers team. Bullying increased to hate mail, death threats, pitchers throwing the ball directly at him, and base runners threatening to spike him. Through it all, Robinson maintained his tongue as well as his courage. He states in his autobiography, *I Never Had It Made*, "I never cared much about acceptance as much as I cared about respect."

Robinson let his playing do the talking. His fame grew to where he earned a batting title as well as the Most Valuable Player award in 1949. The next year, Robinson became the highest paid player in Dodger history, taking home an annual salary of thirty-five thousand dollars!

## Does your belief system damage you?
Anywhere along the way, Robinson could have easily and justifiably adopted a negative belief system. He

could have accepted what others were saying as the truth and concluded that he was a failure. Instead, he knew that failure was an event, not a person. He was not a failure just because he was black or because people didn't like him.

A negative belief system would have held him back by damaging his dreams, goals, or desires. **Is your belief system damaging you?**

Here is one example of how a belief system left unquestioned can cause damage. Were you ever told as a child, "Eat everything on your plate"? I was, and consequently I told my children to do the same. Have you ever wondered where this belief system came from?

Most believe this belief system came from the Great Depression era when people really needed to eat everything on their plates. They didn't know where or when their next meal might come.

Now, in today's age of "super-sizing" and "all-you-can-eat" buffets, Americans are more obese than ever. The old belief system of "Eat everything on your plate," relevant to the Great Depression era, is damaging people today!

Reexamine your belief systems and ask the question, "Is my current belief system supporting my goals and giving me a good quality of life or is it producing negative results and damaging my life?"

Most people form their vocabulary and the manner in which they speak from their belief system. Have you ever noticed the language and speech patterns of someone who had a negative belief system? They are prone to say things like:

- ☐ "I can't believe this is happening to me"

- ☐ "I will never be able to do that"

- ☐ "I am not qualified"

- ☐ "I'm too young"

- ☐ "I'm too old"

- ☐ "I'm not smart enough to do that"

They probably don't even realize it, but everything they speak damages their success. There is so much power in words!

Since we are influenced by our environment, it is safe to say that our parents probably had something to do with establishing our belief systems through words that they spoke into our lives. Negative words produce negative belief systems.

In contrast, if you had parents or other significant individuals who spoke positive words into your life, it impacted your belief system for the better. I had a mother who always spoke positive things over me, saying, among other things, that I would be a millionaire before age thirty.

If I were in line to receive a large inheritance from my parents, that statement would have made much more sense. But, when I was married at age twenty-three, I couldn't even afford our $130 wedding rings. I had to apply three times for a twelve-month term line of credit!

It would have been easy for my mother to give up on me and to recant her statement, but she didn't. She continued to speak millionaire status over my life even when everything around me said that I would be a financial failure. To many people's surprise, before my thirtieth birthday, I had become a millionaire! Thanks, Mom.

Take a minute and ask yourself:

- ❏ How has your belief system affected what you say about yourself?

- ❏ Has it affected what you speak into your children's lives?

- ❏ Has it affected the way you communicate with your spouse or other significant people in your own life?

- ❏ Do you encourage others or do you put them down to subconsciously make yourself feel better?

- ❏ How have positive or negative words impacted your life up until now?

- ❏ Have the words you've been speaking materialized into what you are now living?

Answering these questions will open your eyes to the impact of the words you currently use. If you are pleased with the results, then continue! If you see room for improvement, then it is time to exchange your negative belief system for a positive one and begin using positive words that support the same.

## How to replace a negative belief system with a positive one

To replace a negative belief system with a positive one, you must **#1, <u>examine</u>** each area of your life. If you are being turned away from your dreams, goals, or desires in any particular area of your life, find out why. Is a negative belief system holding you back?

As you examine, look to **#2, <u>identify</u>** the negative belief system. For example, let's suppose that a lack of creativity continually limits your growth in one or more areas of your life. Maybe at work you are denied a promotion because of it. By examining that area, you identify that a negative belief system about your creative ability is adversely affecting you.

*How to do away with a negative belief system:*
*#1-Examine*
*#2-Identify*
*#3-Replace*

Part of identifying the negative belief system is discovering where it came from. You may have had an elementary school teacher who always told you that you were not creative and that you would always struggle with creativity, then, in this example, you know exactly where your negative belief system came from.

The next step is to **#3, <u>replace</u>** your negative belief system with a positive one. You can't just say, "I won't believe that way anymore" and expect lasting change. You must replace that negative belief with a new, empowering, positive one that will move you towards your dreams, goals, and desires. Replacing one for the other will require action and effort on your part.

Continuing with our example, if at work you are faced with an assignment that requires "out of the box" creative thinking, jump in with both feet and take creative action. Associate yourself with other creative people and open your mind to the thought of creativity—**replacing** your negative belief system. Do the best you can and submit the project to your supervisor and expect the best! If your supervisor raves over your work, then you will have broken the barrier!

If not, then use what you learned from the experience and quickly look for another opportunity to grow and expand your creativity.

This may sound odd but remember to speak aloud every day, "I am creative." As you speak it, you will begin to internalize it (whether it is true at the moment or not) and then your behaviors will begin to change to actually reflect what you're speaking.

We generally always believe ourselves, so, as we speak our new beliefs aloud, we begin to believe them. Over time, usually between sixty and ninety days, new habits and beliefs take root based on what we have said and our old negative belief systems are replaced with new positive ones!

## #5—Believing it is impossible

Many, no matter what they are told or what they have seen absolutely believe that it is impossible to be successful. They rationalize, "I don't have the right connections, enough money, or the required raw talent or abilities to ever reach my dreams."

These people usually go through life just taking what life throws at them. They become comfortable and complacent in their day-to-day activities, becoming survivors instead of trailblazers. They are usually risk adverse and try not to "rock the boat." Most do not have a vision for their life yet believe that the world owes them something with an entitlement mentality of sorts.

Proverbs 29:18 explains this as an unhealthy attitude, it states, "Where there is no vision, the people perish." They don't die, they just become unserviceable or of no significant use. Their attitude leads to total loss of significance, which will ultimately give a feeling of no hope or a "what's the use" mentality.

**But with a vision, people find significance!** An envisioned future will keep you going even if you don't have the right connections, money, or raw talent to do it on your own. When you focus on your vision, you will begin to notice opportunities that you never thought existed!

As you begin to talk about your vision, you will begin to attract people who will help you fulfill your vision. Remember, your vision has to always be larger than anything that could pull you away from it—so dream BIG!

If you ever feel like giving up, before you do, take time by yourself and begin to visualize what it will be like a few months or years into the future as you actually begin to attain and live your vision. Don't let today's account of what's happening in your career/life/family/finances discourage you.

As you think about what it will be like when you realize your dreams, goals, and desires, let those thoughts positively pull you through the hard times and keep you moving forward *no matter what!*

A friend of mine, Paul J. Meyer, told me of one of his companies that lost money for nine years. People were telling him to give up and try something else and I'm sure the idea of quitting crossed his mind, but he never did. Today, that same company has recorded worldwide sales exceeding two billion dollars! It is one of the most successful ventures in its field of all time!

Mr. Meyer's envisioned future pulled him through those nine years of losing money to greater success than anyone could have ever imagined. How strong is your vision? How long are you prepared to persevere?

As we set our sights long-term and develop a vision that is large enough to carry us through any bumps in the short-term, success will be inevitable.

What is your vision at this point in your life? Is it crystal clear? Do you have a timeline? What steps are you taking to implement it?

If you can't answer these questions now, don't worry. As we continue to unwrap your gift and as you expand your ideology, we will create a strategy and game plan for its implementation into your life.

Take a look into your future and answer the following questions.

If nothing changes, five, ten, or twenty years from now, where will you be in life? If everything stays the same for the next twenty years, or continues in the same direction, what will you feel like? Are you happy? Sad? Do you feel accomplished?

For most people, that is a depressing thought. The good news is that you can make small changes in your life today that will radically impact your future for the better!

Now, close your eyes and visualize your future **the way you want it.** In this "perfect world" of yours, twenty years from now, . . .

- ❏ Where will you be living?
- ❏ What will your significant relationships be like?
- ❏ Where will you be working?
- ❏ Will you be in good health?
- ❏ How old will you be?
- ❏ What will you weigh?
- ❏ Will you be happy?
- ❏ Do you feel accomplished?

Great! Doesn't that feel better?

Make sure you write your answers in your notebook or journal.

Remember, just as you have the power to visualize a great future, you also have the power and ability to achieve it!

Guess what? You have successfully taken the wrapping off one side of your package! Keep going. Your future is coming into focus and your gift will soon be revealed.

## Chapter Three

# Imagination Precedes Creation
## —You Are What You Think

*W*ith regards to vision, what have you always seen yourself doing that you have not done yet? What has been a desire of your heart that you have not yet acted upon?

If you find it difficult to define your vision, then let's do an exercise that will stir up your creative juices!

Suppose I placed ONE BILLION dollars in your bank account today. That would mean that if you invested it at just 10 percent interest, you would have to spend more than $273,000 dollars each day for the rest of your life *just to spend the interest!*

With this in mind, consider the following:

- ❐ Would you go to work tomorrow at your present job?

- ❐ If you would go to work, would you have a different attitude?

- ❏ What would you begin doing with the money once the excitement wore off?

- ❏ Are there things you have always wanted to do, but lack of money held you back?

- ❏ Now, with no financial concerns, what would you do as an occupation?

- ❏ What would you do as a hobby?

- ❏ How would you help others close to you?

- ❏ Would you live in the same area?

- ❏ Would you associate with the same people?

- ❏ Would those same people associate with you?

- ❏ What would you do with the rest of your life?

I coach so many people who are working from paycheck to paycheck and are unfulfilled in life. They are so preoccupied making a living they don't even think about what they really want to accomplish in their own life.

Most true and lasting success comes when we are doing what we want in life, making enough money to have choices, and enjoying lasting relationships with people who really care. All of these things can be accomplished with the right plan in place, combined with a large dose of good old fashion determination!

## Envision your future NOW

Once you have thought about what you really want to do in life and have answered the questions above, it is very important to keep the proper perspective and mindset. You have probably heard, "You are what you think you are." **Congruent to your success is envisioning yourself becoming the person you want to be.**

Part of becoming the type of person you want requires feeling how it will feel ... right now! What will you feel like when you are actually doing what you love to do, and getting paid for it? How will your relationships improve? What will your new quality of life be like?

Research tells us that when we are not talking out loud, we are constantly talking to ourselves through our own thoughts and meditations. The thoughts we think and the questions we ask ourselves through our internal thought processes become vitally important to our future.

Interestingly, when we ask ourselves the right questions, our minds create the right answers!

For example, if I constantly say, "How did I get so unlucky?" or "Why does this always happen to me?" my mind will give me self-defeating answers. On the other hand, if I ask, "How did I become so fortunate?" or "Why do great things always happen to me?" my answers change! The right answers will lift up and build, rather than degrade and tear down.

Get into a habit of asking yourself the right questions and have faith in yourself that you will come up with the right answers. Don't you remember as a child when our imaginations would "run wild"? We thought about flying, breathing underwater, having x-ray vision, having all the money in the world, et cetera.

What happened?

Through a series of disappointments and with the help of a society that teaches to color within the lines and to not think outside of the box, our imaginations have been squashed! What was once a gift and even an escape from reality has almost turned into a curse.

I've heard people say, "Oh, I could never do that," or "What would people think?" These people have used their imagination to actually cause defeat in their life.

If some of our leading inventors had not possessed a creative imagination, and positive self-talk, where would we be today?

- ❒ We would all be in the dark, without lights or electricity.

- ❒ We wouldn't be able to travel across the country by jet at over five hundred miles an hour.

- ❒ We wouldn't be able to communicate with others around the world by phone or through the Internet.

- ❒ We couldn't watch or record our favorite television shows via cable, satellite, Tivo, or the Internet.

❏ We wouldn't be able to predict weather patterns.

❏ We wouldn't be able to sail across the ocean in "floating hotels" called cruise ships.

❏ We wouldn't have ever walked on the moon or been able to explore other galaxies!

The list goes on and on!

A creative imagination is good. No, a creative imagination is GREAT and absolutely necessary for so many advances in our own lives and in the lives around us! It is the precursor to invention, including the reinvention of yourself! Use your God-given ability to imagine your future so clearly that you actually see yourself there. Meditate on what you want to become and not what you are right now. Ask good questions and begin to experience life exactly the way you want!

You don't even need physical sight to see your future!

## *Ray Charles*

Ray Charles Robinson was born September 23, 1930, in Albany, GA. Like many families during the depression, his family struggled to make ends meet. What's more, by age seven, Ray Charles had lost his sight.

Sent away to the state-supported Saint Augustine School for the Deaf and the Blind, Ray learned to read music with his fingers and write music in braille. Because he couldn't read music and play at the same time, he had to practice until he had it memorized.

He learned to play the clarinet, piano, alto sax, trumpet, and organ. At age fifteen his mother died and Ray left Saint Augustine to pursue his musical destiny. He played at black dance halls around Florida, nearly starving at times. In 1948, wanting to move as far away from Florida as possible, he moved to Seattle.

His first R&B came the next year with "Confession Blues." His own unique sound, a blend of blues, R&B, and gospel, won him twelve Grammy Awards during his lifetime. His musical genius was noticed early and he had several record company contracts and played at the Apollo, Carnegie Hall, and the Newport Jazz Festival.

"I was born with music inside me," he explains. "That's the only explanation I know of . . . music was one of my parts . . . like my blood. It was a force already with me when I arrived on the scene. It was a necessity for me, like food or water."

Being born into the segregated south in 1930 Charles was aware of the evil of racial injustice. Ray Charles knew that since he wasn't able to know when to duck when bottles would be thrown at his head, that it was better for him to help raise money to fight racial injustice. Charles did this for Martin Luther King Jr. and other groups around the world.

Commenting on being black and blind Charles said, "I knew being blind was suddenly an aid. I never learned to stop at the skin. If I looked at a man or a woman, I wanted to see inside. Being distracted by shading or coloring is stupid. It gets in the way. It's something I just can't see."

Having everything seemingly going against him, Ray Charles persevered and continued to "look" where he wanted to go and not where he was, and succeeded.

## Focus on where you want to go

Have you ever wondered how racecar drivers recover from those horrible spinouts and then regain control of their car while traveling at such high speeds? The answer is in where they choose to focus.

They are taught to always look where they want their car to go, NOT where they are going. For example, if their car begins to "spin out" and about to crash into a wall, they are trained to focus at a point on the track where they want their car to go. They are trained to NEVER look at the wall!

The same principle applies in life. Whenever you see yourself spinning out of control, do not look where you are going but begin to focus your efforts on where you want to go. As you focus on where you want to go, even as things around you may be spinning out of control, your life will ultimately follow. Always "see" yourself as a winner, always on top, and always in control.

### Each day is a gift

I once heard of an elderly lady, ninety-two years old, who by 8 A.M. every morning would be fully dressed, hair fashionably done, and makeup perfectly applied . . . even though she was legally blind!

When her husband of seventy years passed away, she moved to a nursing home. During her first day at the home, she was maneuvering her walker to the elevator and the nurse, knowing she was blind, began to describe how her tiny room looked. "I love it," the elderly lady stated with the enthusiasm of an eight year old having just been presented with a new puppy.

"You haven't even seen the room yet," the nurse replied.

"That doesn't have anything to do with it," she replied. "Happiness is something you decide on ahead of time. Whether I like my room or not doesn't depend on how the furniture is arranged, it is how I arrange my mind. I already decided to love it. It is a decision I make every morning when I wake up. I have a choice; I can spend the day in bed recounting the difficulty I have with the parts of my body that no longer work, or get out of bed and be thankful for the ones that do. Each day is a gift, and as long as my eyes open I'll focus on the new day and all the happy memories I've stored away, just for this time in my life."

This little elderly lady used her imagination to dictate her feelings and her feelings dictated what kind of a day she would have. She could "see" even before she saw.

If you are at a point where things don't seem to be working out or if you feel like you're in a holding pattern, remember there are certain seasons in your life for certain reasons. Use what you've learned in each of your experiences to help you progress and ultimately see a brighter future. No matter where you're at now in relationship to where you want to be, continue to "see" the best for yourself and continue to envision the day when you will achieve your goals.

At the beginning of this chapter I asked you to consider several questions, all based on the fact that you had one billion dollars and had to spend $273,000 a day just to spend the interest!

Now, please take a few minutes and answer those questions. After each question, imagine or "see" yourself doing what you would love to do in life. Get vivid and really "see it" in detail. As you are looking at the life of your dreams, please write down what you "see." The more detailed your vision, the better.

- ❏ Would you go to work tomorrow, at your present job?

- ❏ If you would go to work, would you have a different attitude?

- ❏ What would you begin doing with the money once the excitement wore off?

- ❏ Are there things you have always wanted to do, but lack of money held you back? What are those things?

- ❏ Now, with no financial shortage, what would you do as an occupation?

- ❏ What would you do as a hobby?

- ❏ How would you help others close to you?

- ❏ Would you live in the same area?

❐ Would you associate with the same people?

❐ Would those same people associate with you?

❐ What would you do with the rest of your life?

By completing this exercise, you are now one step closer to discovering what's inside your special package. Another piece of wrapping paper has been taken off!

You have also separated yourself even further from the average person. In fact, as you complete each exercise throughout this book, you will be moving towards a ranking in the upper 1 percent of the entire population!

# Chapter Four

# Recognizing Seasons Are for Reasons —Identifying Stepping-Stones to Success

*A*nyone who has achieved any level of significance in life usually has had to overcome obstacles as significant as their achievements! Their obstacles, roadblocks, and challenges turn out to be the very stepping-stones that helped form the pathway to their future!

**One of the most precious gems known to man** is formed when pieces of carbon are pushed together by force and held by pressure. Through that force and pressure the precious diamond is formed. That analogy is so relevant to our own lives, especially when we feel like we've been pushed around or that we are taking on so much pressure that we feel like exploding! Remember that old saying "what doesn't kill you will make you stronger"?

Every time we are faced with the outside pressures of life, remember, a diamond may be forming. Each time we "make it" another day and "get through" what may have caused others to quit, we are forming something more precious than a diamond. We are forming strength, patience, and new skills to use during the next season and for the next steps in our life.

Malcolm Stevenson Forbes insightfully stated, "Diamonds are nothing more than chunks of coal that stuck to their jobs."

## Why resistance is good . . . and necessary

Every time you accomplish "impossible challenges" or press your way through difficult situations, you are becoming stronger. You are preparing yourself for your next steps toward greatness!

> *"Diamonds are nothing more than chunks of coal that stuck to their jobs."*

Ask any bodybuilder or weightlifter and he or she will tell you that the only way to build strong muscles is through resistance.

I know that may sound elementary, but think about it. The only way to make a muscle grow is to put that muscle in a position of needing to resist weight coming against it. Another way to look at it is placing demands on the muscle much greater than it would experience during the normal course of a day. As more demand is placed on any muscle, that muscle will increase its ability to resist. Through that process the muscle actually grows larger as it increases its ability to resist when pressure or additional weight is applied.

**It expands by demand.** As greater demands are required, then it will expand more rapidly to meet the demand—thus becoming larger and stronger.

In fact, the process of expansion involves breakage. Once the muscle is forced to lift additional weights or resist pressure, it actually breaks down and then rebuilds itself stronger. The next time additional weights or pressures are applied; the muscle will be stronger and fully capable to resist whatever comes against it!

You too were born to expand by demand!

This means that we should view pressure as good and even necessary for growth and expansion in our own life. We can actually be thankful for it! We should train ourselves to look beyond our immediate, seemingly negative circumstances and focus on what is actually being formed. The trials we experience are making us stronger!

Just like building muscles, the more demand that is placed on us, the more we learn how to expand, or grow to meet that demand. As we survive and press forward, we come back stronger!

That is why the size of your obstacle means so much. If little demand is placed on you, you cannot grow. If many demands are placed on you, as you meet those demands and handle the pressure, you will literally grow and expand by leaps and bounds.

Think about it. Would you ever allow someone to work on your car that has never had to fix one before? Or, would you ever listen to someone who has never climbed a mountain give you instructions on rock climbing? Why? Because they have never had to expand themselves to meet the demand of the situation.

Have you ever heard the saying, "A hero is always defined by the size of his opponent"? For example, if I am playing one of my out-of-shape neighbors in a game of tennis and I win, it will never mean as much as if I played someone like Andre Agassi or Serena Williams and won!

The greater your opponent, the greater your victory. Likewise, the greater pressure that comes against you in life, the more you grow and expand as you overcome it!

When you adapt this concept to your life, you will begin to welcome challenges and look for opportunities to grow and expand, knowing that you will be stronger as you get through each of them.

## *Earl Stafford*

Founder of Universal Systems and Technology (UNITECH), a leader in net-based training systems, Earl Stafford persevered through some truly adverse circumstances that ultimately gave him a rock-solid foundation and a springboard to unprecedented success.

However, the Stafford household would have told you otherwise at the Christmas of 1990. Earl had just laid off all of his employees, having lost the only two contracts his newly founded corporation had. His business revenue went from a comfortable six figures to zero, literally overnight. He didn't even have enough money to pay his electric bill or buy his children Christmas presents as he had been utilizing all revenue from the business just to keep his employees paid.

But, his entrepreneurial spirit prevailed and his abiding faith to pull himself up by his bootstraps rebounded him from that terrible Christmas.

Stafford eventually landed a lucrative contract with the very company he had lost a contract to three years before. But a lot of sacrifice, hard work, and patience went into those three years.

When UNITECH was hired by NYMA, the corporation that subcontracted for NASA on the Hubble project, Stafford was the president and only employee of his company. The contract demanded a wide assortment of services, from managerial to menial, including some janitorial tasks. Stafford became that janitor by night after working hard all day in a business suit, changing into his work clothes, and picking up the sensitive documentation and cleaning the office spaces that were strewn with paper and debris.

For months, the corporation Stafford contracted with knew nothing, but when word got out that he was also the one cleaning, rather than frowning upon Stafford's work, the company was completely impressed. Stafford's diligence paid off and he was rewarded with a three-year, 2.5 million dollar contract.

Today, Stafford has grown his company back from near insolvency to a forty million dollar company that employs three hundred people. UNITECH currently contracts with the United States military, developing high-tech training software, and has stretched into the private sector through cultivating interactive CD's that teach children about the dangers of drug abuse.

Stafford attributes his ultimate ricochet success to his strong work ethic, a can-do attitude gained from his military experience, and the idea of leading by example. He is a real "get out in front of your troops and refuse to retreat" kind of guy. He never gave up on his dream, risking everything to attain it.

Stafford says, "I love to hear people say, 'I've been safe and secure, but I have this talent, this ability—and it is marketable; I'm stepping out. I might not have all the resources . . . all the wisdom, but I'm going to do it.' Man I really love to hear that."

He encourages others to find their own source of inspiration to tap into when times are tough, to be determined to succeed, and to have enough humility to do whatever victory demands.

It is not surprising that his favorite piece of poetry is from Invictus: "I am the Master of my Fate; I am the Captain of my Soul."

## You CAN overcome!

How many times have you been faced with a seemingly unsurpassable situation, only to ultimately get through it and grow stronger?

Life is full of stepping-stones to greater achievements. The Bible says that as we are faithful over a few things, we will be rewarded with many things. As we take care of what we have now or as we handle what life throws at us, we can move on to greater things.

Unfortunately, many people never handle what they are currently going through. They don't see the light at the end of the tunnel and get caught in the middle of a dark place, wanting to move forward but not being willing to take the necessary steps to get out of their situation.

In our previous book, *Accelerate Your Destiny*, my wife and I show the actual stress test we took during our first year of marriage. On this test, a score of 0-149 means you are moderately stressed, 150-299 indicates that help is needed, and anything over 300 calls for immediate attention. We scored 775! We gave the term "stressed-out" a whole new meaning, but we overcame! As we expanded to meet the demands on our life we became stronger and able to handle nearly anything!

If you are facing a challenge or a dark area in your life, keep reminding yourself:

❏ This will make me stronger!

❏ I will get through it!

❏ I will expand as an individual to meet any demand!

Think of how your current situation will make you expand into someone much stronger. Think of how you'll be able to do more the next time you or someone you love is faced with a similar problem.

Refocus your energies on getting through it instead of getting stuck in it. Just like the race car driver we talked about in the previous chapter, begin looking at where you want to go, NOT where you are going, and you will get to where you want to be!

## ❧ Now It Is Your Turn ☙

Take some time now and reflect on past successes and past failures.

1. List them on a sheet of paper or in your journal.

2. Beside each, list what you learned from the experience.

3. Beside that, list how what you learned may be helping you today, even if in a very small way.

And now for some great news: throughout everything you have read, thought about, and digested up to this point, you have just unwrapped the third side of your package!

# Chapter Five

## *Enlarge Your Borders —Gathering Information for Your Future*

*A*s you begin to make it through the inevitable "tough times," or as we now have learned to say, **"opportunities that will force you to grow and expand,"** what will you need to learn? What knowledge will you need to go to the next level?

For each new endeavor you pursue, there will be a learning curve. The length of that learning curve is largely dependent upon the choices you make:

❐ Will you enroll in a class to learn about your new endeavor?

❐ Will you take a self-study, correspondence course?

❐ Will you obtain a job related to your goal?

❐ Will you model someone?

Let's address the options and look at time frames and possible outcomes.

## Option #1 – Enrolling in a class

If you enroll in a class, please make sure that it will lead directly to accomplishing your goal. Take an extra hour and speak with a counselor or teacher who will be able to tell you exactly what to expect from the class. Once you have clearly communicated your goal, the counselor should be able to explain if the class you're considering is relevant to what you want to accomplish.

Do not be afraid to ask questions. It is better to spend a little time on this up front than it would be to take the class for three, six, or even twelve months and then find out after you have finished that it really was not what you wanted. Preparation and time invested in the beginning will pay big dividends in the end.

## Option #2 – Taking a self-study, correspondence course

If you take a self-study, correspondence course, again, spend time up front ensuring that what you are studying is in line with your goal. There are many scams out there (particularly on the Internet) that promise the moon and very seldom deliver. The old saying, "If something seems too good to be true, it probably is," certainly applies here! Check out the companies very carefully and ask for references that will validate their credibility, then check up on those references!

You must be self-governed and self-motivated to take a self-study course. With no one there to push you, you will need to push yourself and finish in a timely fashion in order to receive any significant benefit. If you have a tendency to procrastinate, I would strongly suggest taking another approach.

## Option #3 – Obtain a job related to your goal

Many people find success by obtaining jobs that ultimately help them achieve their goals in life. You probably will not be able to start out doing exactly what you want, but if you see the promise of "climbing the ladder" to your dream, then finding a position in a field related to your goal is a very good way to uncover your gifts. Just be aware of whom you are working with and of the environment you place yourself in, as this will have a profound influence on your life.

Also, recognize that sometimes working at particular jobs will ultimately prepare you for something totally different. One of my first corporate positions was with Pitney Bowes, a Fortune 150 corporation (one of the largest 150 corporations in America). I knew I did not want to spend the rest of my life selling postage meters, computer manifest equipment, and copiers, but I was being trained for responsibility, trained to make decisions, trained to manage other people, and trained to sell.

After four years, I had worked my way up to a management position within Pitney Bowes and learned how to manage people of all ages. I used many of those same concepts to grow my own company from two employees to more than three hundred! Even though I could not have predicted the future, the position I held at Pitney Bowes groomed me for the next step in my life.

## Option #4 – Modeling someone
Modeling someone means to:

❏ create a relationship with a person who has successfully accomplished what you are endeavoring to do or wish to become and

❏ then use some of the successful techniques you learn to help you reach your own goals.

When sculptors model something, they study their subject very carefully and then slowly begin to create their piece of art. The end product may look similar to what they were studying, but is never identical. The sculptor's own ideas and skills are revealed in each part.

Similarly, when my wife and I decided what we wanted to do in life, we set out on a mission to find the very best model, someone who had successfully implemented what we wanted to do. We then gathered as much information as we could; not to copy, but to help shape what we were creating.

Had we tried to recreate everything without using a successful example or model, we would have wasted a lot of time, effort, and money trying to reinvent the wheel. That is one of the main benefits behind modeling: not having to reinvent the wheel!

Consider gas-powered automobiles. They were created back in the early 1900s, but all of today's cars still use the same type of technology and genius.

While all cars do not look alike or even drive the same way, the same basic principles are still in place. Did you know that the same principles used in a Volkswagen Bug are used in a Porsche, capable of reaching speeds in excess of two hundred miles per hour? As a matter of fact, the Volkswagen was created by Dr. Ferdinand Porsche! Recognize that last name?

You may be wondering just how you are going to get someone successful to be your model. You might even be thinking, "I could never ask someone successful to tell me their secrets or share with me their success." Yes you can!

Allow me to let you in on a little secret: *most successful people LOVE to talk about their successes.*

If you are genuinely interested and will take the time to connect with and develop a sincere relationship, there will be absolutely no problems in finding successful people who will tell you secrets to their successes. Just make sure your intent is pure and that you are not drawn in by their success and begin asking for monetary favors. That is a sure way to kill a relationship. King Solomon, as described in the Old Testament, is one of the richest people to ever exist. The Bible relates that God asked Solomon the ultimate question, "if you could have anything you wanted what would it be?" - Solomon chose wisdom over anything else!

I guarantee you that the right knowledge, coupled with the wisdom to creatively use it, will provide you with an unlimited future! Solomon knew what he was doing!

Find a few mentors, then:

- ☐ model their successful principles,

- ☐ develop great relationships,

- ☐ ask what you can do for them, *and*

- ☐ *watch your future begin to blossom!*

Remember, do not copy, but model them. Allow their ideas and influence to supplement your own creative thinking and ideas.

## The role of visualization

Part of gathering information for your future entails the use of visualization. It ties into successful modeling, finding the right job, taking self-study courses, and even enrolling in a class. *If you can see your future clearly, you are much more likely to live the future you want!*

Not long ago I heard a man speak of how he created one of the largest real estate companies in the nation. He explained that part of his goal-setting procedures included visualizing and taking pictures of the goals he wanted to achieve.

One of his first goals at the beginning of his career was to live in his life-long dream home. He went out and took a picture of what he wanted his dream home to look like. Several years later, he was able to purchase his dream home. Amazingly, when he compared his dream home to the photo he had taken years before, they matched perfectly!

When I worked with Pitney Bowes, we were given specific goals to reach. The company was very smart and sent each employee pictures of things they could win by reaching the goals of the company. *They knew the power of visualization and how it would work!*

One particular year I was given a picture of Hawaii, my reward if I reached a certain goal within the company. Back then I couldn't conceive of actually going to Hawaii, and certainly not on an all-expense paid trip! However, looking at that picture every day before I left the office did something on the inside of me. When I had the choice of going home early or making just one more sales call, that picture of Hawaii would flash before me and compel me to put in one more hour, moving me closer to my goal.

At the end of the year, not only did I qualify to go to Hawaii, but I had made so many sales that I could afford to give my mother something she had dreamed of all of her life—a trip to Hawaii! I can't tell you the feelings I had actually standing in the picture I had looked at so many times before!

## *Colonel David Eberly*

Colonel David Eberly was an American Prisoner of War, shot down during the Gulf War in 1991 by an enemy missile. His story is one of misery, isolation, and starvation at the hands of Saddam Hussein.

In his book, *Faith Beyond Belief*, Eberly describes how he gained faith and focus in life during his experience. As he was tortured, beaten, and constantly moved from camp to camp, he clung to his relentless personal faith.

Eberly recalls how he etched hymn lyrics on a prison wall and how he reflected on childhood memories of his family to endure the terror and hardship of Iraqi captivity. Eberly visualized the number "43" in his mind, and supernaturally knew that he would only have to suffer in captivity for 43 days. Amazingly, this is the number of days Eberly and his comrades were kept by the Iraqi troops.

Colonel Eberly's account is more than courage and leadership—it is an endorsement of the great power that belief and reflection can give to anyone in a time of enormous personal tribulation. Colonel David Eberly went on to win The Distinguished Flying Cross, The Bronze Star, and The Purple Heart awards.

# ❧ Now It Is Your Turn ❧

We have covered many things in this chapter that should be implemented before reading any further. First, fully investigate special courses or classes needed to move you closer to your goals. Check all references and ensure with counselors that the courses under your consideration are exactly what you imagined and will move you directly towards your goals.

Unfortunately, I've seen people actually over prepare and become full-time students. I'm a big proponent of education and think we should never stop learning, *but if learning takes the place of action, then goals are seldom obtained.*

If you want to move things forward a little faster, then you may want to find someone to model. This is a more direct approach but well worth the effort—one of my favorites! Remember, however, that you are looking for someone who has experienced long-term success in many areas of life, not just their occupation. Begin your search now and you won't be disappointed.

Lastly, take steps to visualize your goals. Visualization techniques work only if you take the steps to implement them. Take a break from reading this book and go gather pictures of your goals—things you would like to accomplish in your future. Place these photos somewhere in your home, office, vehicle, or journal so that each day you are forced to look at them.

As you gather information for your future and add the element of the goal you're trying to reach, know that it won't be long until YOU will be standing in that picture, just as I did with my picture of Hawaii. Take down the pictures when you reach your goals and replace them with new ones—new goals! This should develop into a lifelong habit.

Now, one of my favorite parts of this book: if you have completed the exercises above, and all of the others up until this point, let me be the first to congratulate you on removing the fourth side of wrapping paper from your gift!

We're not only about to reveal your gift but if you have been completing all of the exercises at the end of each chapter, you have now separated yourself from 90 percent of the population. You are now ranked in the upper 10 percent of this nation's population!

You ARE completing each exercise, right? Don't let this just be another book to read, but put forth your best effort, follow through, complete your exercises, and take another step towards the life you've always wanted to live.

# Chapter Six

## Faithful Over Few
## —What Have You Done with
## What You Have?

*V*isualization (from the previous chapter) almost places you in a dreamy state of mind whereas you can imagine accomplishing just about anything. Looking at the pictures of your goals on a daily basis is healthy, but do not allow that to distract you from your daily obligations.

As exciting as your goals might be, remember to maintain your current day-to-day activities. There must be balance. Your day-to-day activities are the stepping-stones to get you where you want to go. I once heard that if you keep doing the things you should do, there will come a day when you can do the things you want to do—how true.

As you take care of what is in your hands now, your responsibilities will grow and before long you will have greater things to care for.

## *Bags of gold*

There is a story in the Bible of a certain master who went away on a trip. He left three of his servants various bags of gold to care for, each according to his own ability. The first servant received five bags of gold, the second received two, and the third received one.

When the master returned from his trip, he asked the three servants to give an account of what they had done with his gold:

- ❏ The first servant was proud to say that he had doubled his master's money and turned it into ten bags.

- ❏ The second servant was proud to report that he also had doubled his two bags of gold into four.

- ❏ The third servant explained how he had dug a hole and hid the one bag.

The master suggested that the third servant should have at least put his bag of gold in the bank to gain interest. He called that servant "wicked and lazy" and took the one bag of gold he had and gave it to the servant who had ten bags of gold.

Have you ever heard the saying (particularly from people who have never attained any degree of wealth), "The rich get richer and the poor get poorer"? Under normal circumstances, those who gain wealth are simply more faithful over what is currently in their hands and over time that faithfulness results into greater responsibility, which ultimately results into greater wealth.

What do you have in your hands now that you could be more faithful over or take better care of so that it may grow into something greater?

There are many stories of people who have accepted jobs as cooks—flipping burgers. As they were faithful and flipped a better burger than any of the other cooks, they ended up owning the restaurant!

## From cook to queen

In one of my companies (early learning centers), one particular woman stands out. She was eighteen years old and accepted the position as cook at one of our locations. She was very soft spoken, hardly ever complained about anything, and week after week, month after month, showed up on time and completed all of her tasks better than any cook we had ever employed.

In the grand scheme of things, the position of a cook in that particular industry was considered one of the lowliest positions in the company. It was important (imagine if breakfast or lunch was ever skipped with all those hungry mouths to feed!), but it was still a lowly position.

This young woman could have taken the attitude that the status of her position would determine her faithfulness, but she chose not to. As she remained faithful to that position, it captured my attention. It was obvious to me that she was capable of greater things!

I have always rated employees who possess a great attitude and work ethic over employees with mediocre attitudes and work ethics, independent of their education or experience. I am a proponent of higher education and believe we should never stop learning, but a great attitude and work ethic will always win in the end.

As our cook continued to be faithful, I began to search for positions where she could blossom even further. She ultimately worked her way up to become the director of the entire center, which at that time was the highest position in our company! And on top of that, she was more successful in that position than anyone who had ever held that position. As her responsibilities increased, so did her pay.

Faithfulness does pay off. That same woman, some seven years later, now works with me in some of my current ventures, influencing millions of people all around the world! From humble cook to qualified queen!

Are you working in a lowly position? Are you faithful in that position and have you given it 100 percent on a daily basis? If not, prepare to stay in that same position until you've proved yourself faithful. Worse than that, prepare to be terminated when someone else more faithful is given your position.

If you are being faithful to your position and can honestly say that you are giving it 100 percent every day, it will only be a matter of time until you are noticed. Expect the best as you give your best.

## From bicycles to cars

When my son, Zac, was ready to drive and asked about a car, I was immediately taken back to when he was a small child and received his first bicycle.

As a small child with his first bicycle, he obeyed the parameters we placed on him, proving himself faithful with what he had been given. A few years later, he wanted a minibike (a small version of a motorcycle). Since he had proven himself faithful with his bicycle I had no problem getting him a minibike.

A few years later, he wanted a motorcycle. Even though his mother was not thrilled with the idea, she could not deny the fact that he had been faithful with everything we had tested him with up to that point in time and agreed to the purchase. With his motorcycle, my son changed the oil, kept it clean, and put

> *"There are no secrets to success. It is the result of preparation, hard work, and learning from failure."*
> *- Colin Powell*

on all protective gear each time he rode. He proved that he could handle the responsibility.

When he became of age to drive and began to ask about a car, my wife and I were both prepared to help him purchase the best he could afford. Our deal with him was to match each dollar he saved towards his new vehicle and when it came time for him to drive, we would help with half of the purchase.

Once again, he faithfully saved his money and was able to purchase a one-year-old Chevy Tahoe in excellent condition. With the money he had left, he purchased custom tires, lifted the body, and upgraded the stereo. Some of his classmates were saying how lucky he was, but luck had nothing to do with it. Faithfulness, coupled with a great attitude and work ethic, prevailed!

The key ingredient to "being faithful over few" is diligence and hard work.

Hard work does not begin when success arrives. *Success is birthed by hard work, perseverance, persistence, and stick-to-it-iveness.*

As you are faithful over the less-than-glamorous job you might have now, remember to work hard everyday, even if you do not feel like it. Your co-workers might be the worst on the planet and you might get paid much less than you deserve, but always remember: no one was ever promoted for complaining, not showing up for work, or for having a bad attitude.

Begin preparing for your success today!

## *Gregory Peck*

Gregory Peck is considered by many to be one of the all-time best actors. He is perhaps best known for his award-winning portrayal of Atticus Finch in *To Kill A Mockingbird*.

What most people have never learned is that Peck worked his way through college as a bus boy, a waiter, a parking lot attendant, and a janitor. "I've always believed that you must work for what you achieve. I never felt it was a hardship," he says. "I learned that early and it served me well."

Peck studied at a drama school for two years, then he worked in summer theaters and with touring companies. He worked hard at small roles in forty plays before he was selected for his first Broadway part.

"I never had any other idea but that you had to work if you wanted to achieve something. That was the thread that ran through my life," Peck explains, adding, "Use yourself as well as you can and be the best that you are in your work."

Stay faithful with what you have now. If it is a job, work harder at that job than anyone else. If it is a car, take care of it as if it was worth a million dollars. If it is a home, make sure that the yard is mowed, windows cleaned inside and out, and everything is in good repair.

Whatever the example, begin being faithful over everything you have and I promise the time will come when you will be promoted and rewarded with more!

Take a blank piece of paper and write, "Faithful over what I have now," across the top of it. Then draw two vertical lines equally spaced on the paper, from top to bottom, giving you three columns on the paper under the title.

Then, in the left-hand column, list your current possessions, job, friendships, financial status, et cetera. In the middle column, write down what you desire in the future pertaining to each of your current possessions.

For example, if you currently live in a three-bedroom, 1,500-square-foot home, but are aiming for a larger one, you would write "1,500-square-foot home" in the left-hand column and "3,000-square-foot home" in the middle column.

In the right-hand column, write down what you could be doing NOW, per each item, to become more faithful as you work towards your goals.

On the same line that you listed your 1,500-square-foot house, what could you begin doing today to take better care of what you have?

When you complete your list, place it somewhere visible so that it constantly reminds you of where you are now and where you are going. Your hard work, dedication, and faithfulness with what you have now will eventually pay off big!

Congratulations on removing the fifth side of paper from your gift! Are you getting excited to see what's inside?

# Chapter Seven

## Chart a New Course
## —Creating Your Own Master Plan

*I*t is now time to actually chart the course for your master plan for success! I guess you could say this is where the rubber meets the road. Having a plan is so important, yet studies indicate that less than three percent of the population actually has one!

Caution—by the end of this chapter, if you do not take the steps to create your very own plan for your life, you will rank with 97 percent of the population who do not have a plan, do not get results, and never live the life of their dreams. Conversely, if you do finish this chapter, complete the exercises and develop a life plan (I know you will!) you will be ranked among the upper 3 percent of the population who truly live the life of their dreams!

If you have made it this far in the book, you have already proven your "faithfulness to a task." You possess what it takes to complete this chapter and create your very own master plan for success. Congratulations!

Now, let's get started. To create a master plan, you will need to use some of the information you've already discovered about yourself in the previous chapters of this book.

Remember what you identified in chapter three—that "thing" you would do if money were no object? This should be something that you love to do and could see yourself doing for the rest of your life, with or without pay!

Perhaps that "one thing" has changed a little, or a lot, since you've read the subsequent chapters. If so, pull out your journal or your notes and write down your new goal(s). For maximum effectiveness, try to limit your answers to no more than three, as you will ultimately be asked to focus in on one primary goal.

Focus will be a key in the successful formation and implementation of your life plan. Sometimes people with great ideas, dreams, and goals never accomplish anything because they don't focus on any one thing long enough to complete it. Having too many goals is like having none at all.

### *Laser focus*

I was in a sales meeting a few years ago in Hawaii and witnessed one of the most powerful examples of focus that I've ever seen. We were all in a large room and all the lights went out! It was pitch black. Then suddenly, hundreds of laser beams began to shoot out from a light that appeared in the center of the room. It looked almost like a strobe light, except with laser beams dancing across the auditorium.

Then a narration began in the background and a man's voice said, "A laser beam, when broken up, is very weak (as the audience watched hundreds of lasers dance across the auditorium), but when a laser is FOCUSED, it can cut through metal!"

When the narrator said the word "focused," all the lasers came together to form one of the brightest single beams of light that I've ever seen!

It was at that moment that everyone in the room realized that when we spend our time chasing many different things each day and utilize only a fraction of our energy and focus on each, we are never as effective as when we focus 100 percent on that "one thing!" Once we focus all of our energies on that "one thing," our dreams begin to transform into realities.

The following exercise is one of the most important ones in this book. It will bring that "one thing" in your life into focus and teach you specific steps to take in its' implementation.

# ❧ Now It Is Your Turn ☙

This chapter is particularly short for a reason. Destiny, purpose, significance, dreams, goals, and desires are personal and different for everyone. I do not want to write too much about your specific dream and inadvertently influence it. My goal is to motivate you just enough so that your own thinking motivates you to take action.

Please open your journal (hopefully you are using one by now—I don't want to see you as part of the 97 percent of the population who doesn't follow through) and write down one specific thing that you've only dreamed of in the past. That "one thing" you would do if you had a billion dollars in your bank account.

Take your time and write down as much detail about that "one thing" as you can. Paint the perfect picture with words and be specific. For example:

- ❑ I will open a car dealership in my home town and sell exotic cars, specifically, Porsches, Ferraris, and Lamborghini's.

- ❑ I will try and locate in a particular area of town.

- ❑ I will hire two people to start with—maybe Bill and Sue.

- ❑ I will talk to three successful people about the success they've had in the same field and gain valuable insight.

- ❑ Before talking to my banker, I will create or get help in creating the perfect business plan.

After you have completed this exercise, let's start envisioning your future. Whatever your goal, write down how you are going to feel when you accomplish it. What will your day by like when you're doing what you've always wanted to do? How will it affect your attitude? How will you feel about yourself? How will others perceive you? How will your energy level be affected? Please take the time to write each answer in your journal.

How does it feel to actually see your dream begin to materialize? Are you having any anxieties? When you see your dream written down with details, does it give you a warm feeling inside or are you getting sweaty palms?

Any type of reaction is good—that means you are emotionally attached to your dream. Why shouldn't you be? You were born with this and now you are about to birth it into reality.

When an expectant mother carries her baby for just nine months, she instinctively becomes very attached even though she has never seen it. How long have you been carrying your baby?

Have you ever written down this dream before? If so, what happened? If your dream has not yet been achieved, take comfort in the fact that by the time you are finished with this book, you will be well on your way to accomplishing it.

Together, we will experience the birthing of your baby. This is a new day and the slate has been wiped clean. This time you will succeed! You are now ready for success! You won't have to spend another day of your life wondering, "what if ...?"

As we go through this exercise together, to help ensure optimal success, make a special effort to maintain a positive mental attitude, remaining in a state of positive expectancy. Only expect the best. Just like a camera, what you focus on will ultimately develop. Just like the racecar driver, continue looking where you want to go, not where you've been.

Whenever I do this exercise, I always save what I have written down and review it sometime in the future, no matter how outlandish it may have sounded at the time I wrote it down. I'm always pleasantly surprised at the outcome.

One of my favorite poems by Guillaume Apollinaire says:

> *"Come to the edge" he said*
> *They said, "We are afraid"*
> *"Come to the edge" he said*
> *They came*
> *He pushed them . . .*
> *And they flew*

Now, please set this book down and take at least thirty minutes **today** of uninterrupted quiet time and think about your dream—that "one thing." You will want to take your journal so you can keep track of your thoughts.

Go somewhere peaceful and quiet. Allow your dream to begin to grow. Remember everything we have talked about up to this point as your dream begins to come into perfect focus. Think of all the possibilities and prepare to FLY!

If you haven't actually completed the exercises up to this point in the book, please do not go any further. The base we have just established will be used in the remaining chapters. Please do yourself a favor and complete the exercises. Use the positive momentum now established to successfully complete your own master plan for success and begin living the life of your dreams!

If you have completed each exercise up to this point, then it is with great honor and respect that I now congratulate you on removing the lid to your gift! YES!!!

You should be able to see it now, how exciting! Savor the moment.

As a bonus you have also just separated yourself from the other 97 percent of the population who never get this far in creating a life plan!

Throughout the next chapter, we will carefully take your gift out of the box and learn the steps necessary to implement it into your everyday life.

# Chapter Eight

## Implement Your Plan
## —Action Steps to Success

*Y*ou have now reached the implementation phase. In getting this far, you are now ranked in the upper 3 percent of the population! How does it feel? The habits you have created thus far in completing each exercise will be the same habits that keep this positive momentum going for the rest of your life. Congratulations!

Now that you have removed all the wrapping paper and can see your gift, let's discuss how to put it into practice.

### Time for show and tell

Now that you have unwrapped your gift, it's only natural to want to show it off. Who will you show or who will you tell about your gift? As odd as this may sound, you will need to be very careful in selecting who to share this information with.

Have you ever bought something new or received a promotion at work and told someone, only to discover that the person you told really was not that happy for you? Even worse, have you ever told anyone about something good that happened in your life, only to find that it created jealousy?

Everyone will NOT be as excited as you are right now about your gift. That's okay! In fact, it is usually not a good idea to talk to everyone about it anyway.

When I first began to discover my gift, I was so incredibly excited! I started telling everyone, whether

> **Action Step #1:**
> **Decide who you will**
> **show your gift to.**

they wanted to hear it or not, about my dreams, goals, and desires. I thought that just because it was clear to me, it would be clear to them and they would

naturally share in my excitement. Nothing could have been further from the truth!

Most of the people I told began to grumble and complain, saying things like: "Who does he think he is?" or "He'll never be able to do that!" or "How does he think it is even possible?"

They did not share in my excitement! In fact, they tried to do the opposite and quench my excitement with their negative comments.

I discovered that most people did not understand or could not comprehend me because **my gift was not their gift**. It was mine! They could not "get it" like I had.

The same applies to you. No one on earth possesses the exact same gift as you. They may have similar gifts, but your gift is uniquely yours and yours alone. Gifts are not "one-size-fits-all." It is a tragedy to watch people try and copy someone else's gift. It wastes time, energy, talent, and money.

Carefully select the right people to tell about your gift. Resist the temptation to tell the world.

## Search for success

Once you have discovered your gift and know beyond a shadow of doubt that this is where you will be focusing your time, energy, and resources, the next step is to find someone who has already succeeded. Look for someone who has similar gifts and has experienced great success. Again, DO NOT COPY, but learn and use some ideas,

> *Action Step #2:*
> *Find someone who has already succeeded.*

along with your own, to move you closer to the realization of your own goal.

When searching for someone with a similar gift, someone who has already succeeded in what you want to do, make sure you do your homework. Find out if that person has been successful for a long period of time and if others in the same field can validate your findings. If you're going to spend the time and effort to study and learn from someone else, you might as well study from the best and the most successful!

Surprisingly enough, you will find that most successful people really enjoy talking about what made them successful. If you don't pose a threat and your approach is done with style and in taste, just about anyone will talk to you. Many people get intimidated about calling or visiting with highly successful people, but there is really nothing to fear. They want to tell you about themselves if you will listen.

Finding incredible success, based off of the success of someone else, is not new. It is often the basis for new inventions, new companies, and new breakthroughs. A good example is Wal-Mart. In 1962, business-minded Sam Walton heard of a new discount store opening in Chicago called, "Kmart." Sam studied it and then replicated it. Thirty years later, upon his death, Sam Walton's fortune was estimated at twenty-eight billion dollars!

As my wife and I developed our business, we relentlessly pursued others who were successful at what we wanted to develop. We found that if successful people were approached the right way, they would be happy to share their story. (We made some very good friends along the way.)

We combined everything we discovered with our own ideas. As a result, our business gained the reputation as one of the best in the industry, growing from two employees to more than three hundred.

## Reevaluate & clarify

After you have spent time looking at other businesses in the same or similar field and interviewing other successful individuals, reevaluate your goal.

Ask yourself if your goal is still something that you want to pursue. Has your perception changed since you began your investigation? Don't be afraid to change, but are you as sure as you were when you first started?

If so, then be true to yourself. Make sure your goal always remains your goal and don't

> ### Action Step #3:
> ### Reevaluate and clarify
> ### your goal.

allow anyone or anything to dissuade you. Clarify your goal even further. Let your passion burn even brighter. Allow yourself to become even more excited than before!

## Time your grand entrance

With a clarified goal and excess excitement, it is tempting to neglect everything else and focus 100 percent on your goal. Though enticing, this is a dangerous point for many people. Until the implementation of your gift is producing enough cash flow to cover your current income, **don't quit your day job!**

If you are financially able to take that course of action, fine. However, if you are like most of the population who work for a living, then you need to maintain your primary job until your new venture begins to pay off.

When I first began using my gifts towards my career goals, I felt like I was leading a double life. I remained at my primary job to keep food on the table for my family, but almost every other waking moment I was thinking about and taking steps towards my newfound goal. When the income from my new goal exceeded the income from my current position, I knew it was time to resign. It was a great day when I could actually spend 100 percent of my time on what I enjoyed doing! The timing worked out perfect!

It may be hard to control the urge to jump in before the time is truly perfect, but you must not let your emotions drive you into a state of poverty. The success or failure of most new ventures is normally based on adequate capitalization or

> **Action Step #4:**
> *Time your grand entrance!*

as some people say: money! If you haven't saved enough money to put into the business or new idea to keep the momentum moving forward while simultaneously keeping food on your table, then you may want to reconsider your timing.

When you finally resign your day job, please remember to do it gracefully. You'll never know when or where you may run into your supervisors or co-workers. I have crossed paths many times with people that I used to work with, and many of them have helped and supported me because of how I treated them during my tenure and more importantly upon my resignation.

If you ever employ others, good business practices will become even more important. It all comes down to treating others like you want to be treated.

## Developing a plan

If reaching your goal requires you to start a new business, one of the first steps to take should be the completion of a thorough business plan. There are many small business leaders and agencies that would love to help. One of the greatest resources that I've used in the past is my banker.

Since your new venture will probably require money and since you most likely will visit your local banker, why not have him working with you from the beginning?

Two of the primary ways that a bank makes money is by producing quality loans and receiving deposits. In order to help your banker accomplish that goal, you must first qualify for a loan. Bankers want you to qualify and will generally work with you to do so. Once you have qualified, they will probably ask for your deposits as

> *Action Step #5:*
> *Develop your plan!*

well. Please understand, your success is part of their success.

I remember visiting about seven or eight banks when I began my first business. Every banker I spoke with told me why I couldn't qualify. Finally, I asked one banker to tell me how to qualify instead of listing all the reasons why I couldn't. I asked for a list of things I needed to do and received his commitment that if I accomplished everything on that list, he would loan me the money. It was then that he really helped me pull everything together and ultimately financed my first project.

## On the same page

As your vision develops, you will want to make sure that you are on the same page with your key players (spouse, significant other, business partner, et cetera). The principle that "a house divided against itself cannot stand" applies to every endeavor. For those who are married, if you have two visions, then division is created which usually leads to divorce.

Married couples, make sure you are not only on the same page, but in the same book! As you communicate your likes and dislikes, wants, needs, dreams, goals, and desires, always work towards

> **Action Step #6:**
> **Get on the same page!**

a win-win situation. That way you are always in agreement and on the same page.

One important principle to consider is that even if you disagree with your spouse, significant other, or business partner, always show support for their decisions in front of those who work with you. Discuss differences in private, because if you don't, the lack of support within upper-level management will discredit the entire organization. **Supporting your partners in public and discussing differences in private are key ingredients for a healthy organization.**

## Recruiting others to join you

As your goal begins to come into reality, you may need to recruit others to join you. As you ask others to join you, A) let go of any pride that may exist and B) try to recruit up (look for people smarter than you).

Humility is required. Remember, a plane is never on course 100 percent of the time. The pilot is constantly adjusting for crosswinds, turbulence, or storms. Once you begin moving towards your goal, you must keep adjusting until you succeed. Never be afraid to regroup, try something new or adjust as you move forward.

> ### *Action Step #7:*
> ### *Look for others to help you!*

Always keep your eyes open for talented people who possess the ability to see your vision and may want to join your team. Remember, the better your help, the faster you can reach your goals!

## Establish a support group

As you move through difficult times it's very important to establish a support group. A healthy support group will get you through difficult times that others may not have the capacity to endure. Friends and family are very important and need to be kept abreast of your new developments and should always offer support. However, if someone outside of your immediate family (wife or children) does not understand your vision and becomes more of a hindrance to your progress, you may want to limit the exposure you give them to

> ### *Action Step #8:*
> ### *Establish a support group.*

your new idea. Surround yourself with those who will support and not try to tear you down.

## Choose to succeed

The next step is to choose to succeed. Don't get me wrong. This is no flippant, "Well, okay, I guess I will" type of choice. No, this is a choice that requires constant choosing!

Choosing to succeed has requirements, including:

## 1—A crystal clear vision

If you cannot describe your goal in detail to someone in less than one minute, then your goal is probably not clear enough. If you have doubts in your own mind or simply cannot quite see the whole picture, then you need to spend extra time redefining your goal.

## 2—A pit bull mentality

Have you ever wondered how the pit bull got its reputation as one of the fiercest fighting dogs ever? There is something bred inside most pit bulls that causes them to have such determination as to never let go, no matter what.

Once the pit bull has sunk its teeth into something, it doesn't let go! This breed of dog has learned over the years that if it bites down and holds on just one second longer than its opponent, it will win.

When talking to people about your dreams, goals, and desires, you need a pit bull mentality so that no matter what they say to you or about you, you continue on. You have bitten down and sunk your teeth into a crystal clear vision, and you will not let go until you succeed!

## 3—100 percent commitment

Once the goal is defined, your commitment level must register at 100. If you are not ready to commit your time, energy, and money to the attainment of your goal, then you may need another goal.

> ***Action Step #9:***
> ***Decide that you are***
> ***going to succeed!***

When my own goal came into focus, I remained at my "day job" to put food on the table for my family, however, 100 percent of all my free time was directed towards my newfound goal.

Doing this for too long will result in an unbalanced life and could affect your health and important relationships, but sometimes short-term sacrifices must be made to accomplish long-term success.

## 4—Stand strong

If you hit a wall, don't stop. Stand strong, but do find out what type of wall it is. Can you go over it, under it, or through it? There is a way, so keep looking until you find it.

By standing strong, you become a better person, you learn new skills, you meet new people, and you prepare yourself for even greater success. You will succeed!

I've talked to many people who have given up on their dreams at one time in their life and in retrospect have never forgiven themselves for doing so. If you have given up on a dream remember, as long as you have breath, it is not too late! You can never be too old.

## *Colonel Sanders*

At age sixty-five, Colonel Sanders found himself living from paycheck to paycheck on just $105 per month from social security. Something changed on the inside. He decided this was not the life he was going to lead.

He took action and began selling chicken with his "special recipe" for just five cents per piece ... from the trunk of his car! Then he started to visit restaurants and try to convince them to sell his chicken. Today there are more than one billion Kentucky Fried Chicken dinners served per year in more than eighty countries!

What if Colonel Sanders had listened to what others were saying about him? Just think if he would have given up and said, "They are right. I'm too old and too crazy to pursue my dream."

Instead, he chased his dream until he caught it! I wonder how large KFC would have grown if he would have started at age fifty-five?

## Readjust until you reach your goal

Sometimes once you've started taking steps towards your goal, adjustments need to be made and processes need to be recalculated. Unfortunately some people think their way is the only way, no matter what the outcome. The definition of insanity is doing the same thing over and over, but expecting different results. A fly can only hit a window so many times trying to get out before it's either knocked out, dies of exhaustion, or gets smart and finds another door or window to exit.

In many ways we are the same way. Our goal may not need to change—like the fly trying to get out, but our process may need to be adjusted. Sometimes we should be looking for another window or door to go through! Always ask questions and examine every possibility towards the attainment of your goal. If one thing doesn't seem to be working, reevaluate, ask other successful people, adjust for crosswinds and storms, and then keep flying until your goal is reached!

> *Action Step #10:*
> *Readjust until you*
> *reach your goal.*

# ⮐ Now It Is Your Turn ⮑

It's really all up to you now—you have been shown the door, but it's up to you to open it. The chapters you've read and the exercises you've completed have all been stepping-stones to get you to this point—where your gift is revealed!

Please reread this entire chapter and mark the places that call for action on your part, and as Nike says "just do it!" Remember to:

1. Decide who you will show your gift to.
2. Find someone who has already succeeded.
3. Reevaluate and clarify your goal.
4. Time your grand entrance.
5. Develop your plan.
6. Get on the same page with your partners.
7. Look for others to help you.
8. Establish a support group.
9. Decide that you are going to succeed.
10. Readjust until you reach your goal!

Just as in previous chapters, if you have taken the time and thoroughly completed each exercise at the end of every chapter, let me be the first to congratulate your efforts and announce to the world that YOUR GIFT HAS NOW BEEN REVEALED!!!

You are on your way to such a great future; I'm so excited for you!

The next three chapters will add the finishing touches to this entire process and help ensure long-term, balanced success. They will also show you how to move from your current 3 percent ranking in society to the upper 1 percent of the population!

## Chapter Nine

# *Measuring Progress*
## *—Inspect versus Expect*

*M*easuring your progress is an integral part of reaching your goal. Someone once told me that people will seldom do what you expect but will generally always do what you inspect! How true.

As a rule, we procrastinate whenever possible. If a person is not held accountable to a specific time frame to accomplish certain tasks, things generally will not get done.

Why do you think the longest lines of the year develop at post offices in the United States on April 15—tax day? Lines actually get longer as the clock approaches midnight! The reason is that midnight, April 15, is the deadline to file a tax return in the United States without an extension.

We are given a deadline that we have nearly twelve months to prepare for, yet the vast majority of the population waits until the last minute! Why? Usually because of procrastination.

## The power of deadlines

Why do you sometimes see people running in airports? Usually it's because they are rushing to get on a plane before it takes off. A deadline was set for the plane to take off and history tells us that planes do not wait. If word ever got out that a plane would wait no matter how late you were, schedules in airports would cease to exist. Even people I know who are usually late to everything are never late for their flight. Why? Because a time frame was set with no options for change. If you miss the flight, you will generally lose your ticket and your travel plans are either severely hindered or cancelled completely.

Who sets the time frames for us in everyday life? Usually it is our boss or supervisor at work. If we adhere to those time frames and accomplish what is expected of us, we can expect to keep our jobs. If we disregard the time frames and requirements, then we can expect to lose our jobs to someone who will get the job done within the time allotted.

In sales, time frames generally occur on a monthly basis. Consider Bob, the typical salesperson. At the beginning of each month, there is a big zero next to his name indicating a fresh start with no sales. As the month progresses Bob tracks along until he realizes that the last week is quickly approaching and he is no where near his goal! Now, panic time sets in! Suddenly Bob has no trouble getting out of bed early each morning or even working a full eight to ten-hour day! He charges toward his goals with focused deter- mination.

Why do we do this to ourselves? Because the end is near and we can clearly see the relationship between the time frame set before us, the time we have left, and what still needs to be accomplished! Imagine if Bob worked the entire month as hard as he did the last week in each month!

The same phenomenon occurs when we take vacations. A few days before it is time to leave, panic begins to set in. You start to wonder if you've made enough lists for the people who will assume your duties. Are all the bills paid and current? Is the yard mowed? Who will take care of the animals? What about the mail? Who will pick up the paper? The list goes on and on!

What would our lives be like if we lived each day like it was the day before we were to go on vacation? How productive would we be? How much more could we accomplish?

## Learn to set your own deadlines

Setting time frames and goals to accomplish within those time frames are paramount to any level of success. In fact, if time frames are not set, most goals will never be accomplished.

## Hawaii

Whenever I worked for a Fortune 150 corporation, as I've previously discussed, a goal was placed before me to sell a certain amount of products in one year. Upon accomplishing this goal, I could qualify for an all expense paid trip to Hawaii. This was huge for me. Up until that time in my life I didn't even know how to pronounce Hawaii, let alone think I would ever go there!

I did something that year that no one else in the office did and that was to make a chart (resembling a thermometer) of where I was now and where I wanted to be by the end of the year.

Because the end of the year was so far away, I broke the chart down into daily sales. Each time I would make a sale; I would come into the office and color in the level of sale I made. This way I could immediately see how close each sale put me in relationship to the trip to Hawaii I was trying to win. Every morning before I left the office I would take a good look at that chart and knew that when I came back to the office at the end of the day, I would either be coloring in the chart as a success or walking away as a failure.

To make a long story short, by the end of the year, as we were only a few weeks away before the contest ended, the other salesman in the office began to cheer me on. They too could see my progress and even felt part of it by now. As the last days approached, I finally made enough sales to qualify for the trip to Hawaii for me and my entire family! What a great day. And since I had made so many sales to qualify, I had money to spend as well—a double blessing!

There is so much power and positive momentum created when we set goals and time frames. So why do most of us still procrastinate? Why aren't all of our goals met? Until we develop a positive infrastructure in our lives—someone or even a group of people that will both support our efforts and help hold us accountable to the changes necessary to reach our goals—we'll continue to have a hard time attaining anything in life.

## Coaching

One of the most common reasons goals are not achieved seems to stem from whether or not a person is held accountable to their actions as they relate to obtaining their goals. Coaching, which is near and dear to my heart, seems to be one of the most consistent systems in helping individuals and businesses obtain goals. As an unbiased third party, a coach has the ability and advantage of standing outside of the forest so that he or she can see the trees.

People usually think of coaching as it relates to sports. A sports coach, in any discipline; be it basketball, football, baseball, soccer, et cetera, trains players under his or her tutelage to win. The coach is normally not a player, but rather imparts his knowledge that will enable each player to operate at peak performance and win.

The coach will never be the player's sole resource, but will enable each player to become resourceful, using what they have been taught to excel on the field. The coach is not always the most popular person on the team either, but he is able to push the players to reach levels that they didn't think they could reach given their individual skill set!

## Bear Bryant

"Bear" Paul William Bryant earned his nickname by wrestling a bear in a theater. Bear Bryant was a great American college football coach who retired with a record 323 coaching victories. He was the head coach at the University of Maryland in 1945, the University of Kentucky from 1946 to 1953, Texas A&M University from 1954 to 1957, and the University of Alabama from 1958 to 1982.

After becoming an all-state football player in high school, Bryant played college football for the University of Alabama and became an assistant coach there after graduation in 1935. When he secured his first head-coaching job at Maryland after World War II, he acquired a reputation as a demanding coach and strict disciplinarian. In 1946, he moved to Kentucky, taking the UK team to four bowl games. At Texas A&M, Bryant won the Southwest Conference championship in 1956.

Returning to Alabama in 1958, he revitalized the football program and in 1961 had the nation's top-ranked college football team. His 1964, 1965, 1973, and 1978 teams were also ranked number one in one or more polls, and his 1979 team was the only one to be ranked first unanimously in the postseason polls. Under Bryant, Alabama had twenty-five winning seasons and was selected for bowl games twenty-four times!

## Tom Landry

Tom Landry was another famous coach, responsible for taking the legendary Dallas Cowboys to numerous wins and super bowl victories. **"Setting a goal is not the main thing. It is deciding how you will go about achieving it and staying with that plan,"** he is quoted as saying. **"Leadership is getting people to do what they don't want to do, to achieve what they want to achieve."**

As you can see, these great coaches did nothing more than pull the best out of the people they worked with . . . and literally became famous as a result!

## Perform at your peak!

Have you ever stopped and thought of why millions of people pack arenas and stadiums each year at athletic events? It is because people will pay to see someone performing at their peak, operating in their gift—doing that "one thing" they love!

Most athletes are quick to give credit to their coaches. They often explain that even when they wanted to give up, their coach helped push them through hard times and held them accountable to the changes necessary to reach their goals . . . ultimately becoming ALL they could become!

One of the greatest coaches in golf is David Leadbetter. Although he has one of the best track records as a golf coach, you will never see his name associated with winning tournaments. Why? Because he expends his energies on coaching, not playing. Research tells us that a coach doesn't necessarily need to be superior in what he or she is coaching, just able to look at the big picture and get results.

Leadbetter can take a step back and give each of his "major tournament winning" clients a different perspective on their swing, and for that matter, their entire game. Like I've said previously, he takes a step outside of the forest to get a different look at the trees. As a result, most professional golfers consider him as one of the greatest coaches of all time.

Why don't we all have coaches to help us reach beyond ourselves? If we want to play the piano, we hire a piano coach. If we want to learn to sing we hire a vocal coach. If we want to become better at just about anything, coaching seems to be the answer.

What great advancements could be made if we began a relationship with a life or business coach? Even those who are the best in their field continue to retain two and sometimes three different coaches, keeping them on top of their game! Peak performers!

I have often pondered the fact that as a nation we will invest in our cars to make sure they operate at peak performance and invest billions in weight loss programs to make sure the outside of our bodies look good. However, when it comes to investing in ourselves, examining how and why we make certain decisions, we sometimes stop.

This subject matter deserves an entire book by itself. However, for the sake of time, if you are interested in obtaining more information about personal or business coaching, please refer to the information page on life and business coaching located in the back of this book.

## Inspect your own progress

Another great way to stay accountable to a task within a certain time frame is to inspect your own progress on a daily basis. Remember the Hawaii trip? I'm convinced that the thermometer chart I made and looked at on a daily basis, morning and night, was very instrumental in the attainment of my goals.

Whatever your goal, you should be able to reduce it to writing, chart it, and measure it. Whether it is losing weight, running long distances, lifting weights, increasing sales, or spending more time with your family, EVERYTHING can and should be measured.

I recently started running. During my first week, it looked more like walking, but at least I was making the effort. After about two months of working my way up to longer distances within certain time frames, I saw an ad for a "runners watch" and ordered it. Upon receiving this watch I learned just how many ways my running could be measured—it was amazing. Even more amazing was the very first day I began using this watch and measuring my progress, all my times improved. As I ran, I continued to think about the fact that I was being measured. Every time I thought of slowing down or just walking, the thought of being measured kept me going! This concept works in every area of life, if you put the concept to work.

Please do not pass this section by without stopping to create something that can be used to measure your progress towards whatever goal you have identified. Anything you want to improve, begin measuring it and watch it naturally begin to improve!

## Find a mentor

One final way to measure your progress and have others help hold you accountable is to find a mentor. A mentor can open your eyes to new ideas and help hold you accountable to the change necessary to accomplish your goals.

Please make sure, as we have already discussed, that your mentor has experienced success in the same area that you are pursuing and that he or she maintains a balance in other areas of life as well. Your mentor does not have to be perfect, but you wouldn't want to be mentored by someone who may be successful in business but has neglected his or her family or other significant relationships. I would hate to be known as a public success and a private failure!

Find someone who has balanced, long-term success, and has walked their talk. I have been fortunate enough to call Mr. Paul J. Meyer my friend, but more importantly my mentor. To actually find someone who walks their talk, and then some, is very unusual but vitally important to your long-term success.

To review, create a way to both display your goal and track its progress.

Next, find a life or business coach you trust. Since coaching has become such a phenomenon, people everywhere are trying to jump on the bandwagon and call themselves a coach. Use your intuition, choose carefully, and check references—you will be glad you did!

Lastly, find a mentor you can look up to and learn from. This may be a relative, a boss, or someone you have admired for a long time. But again, enlist someone with a proven track record who is balanced, successful, and seasoned.

MEASURING
PROGRESS

GOAL

# Chapter Ten

## Life in Balance
## —Building Legs under Your Table

Seeking to live a balanced life is one of the most significant decisions you'll ever make. For that reason, you will want to read and reread this chapter many times as a reminder to live your life in balance.

A study was conducted by *Fortune* magazine on the chief executive officers of the largest five hundred corporations in America. The question was asked of each of them, "If you could change anything about your tenure as a Fortune 500 CEO, what would you do differently?"

Amazingly, nearly 80 percent said they would have spent more time with their families.

To make this point clear, imagine your life as a table. Men, I'm sure you are thinking of a big, thick, walnut, or oak table, capable of holding anything! Women, if you are anything like my wife, you may be envisioning something a little daintier and certainly more stylish. Regardless of the table, it must have legs for support; otherwise it isn't a table at all, it's just a piece of material lying on the floor!

The more legs you have under your table, the better the support. How hard would it be for a table of any size, style, or shape to stand on just one leg? Imagine how wobbly it would be. What if that leg was ever broken or kicked out from under the table? You're right; the table would fall because it was relying on just one leg for support.

Likewise, your table of life must have a healthy support structure (many strong legs) to hold it up. I have found that just about everyone's table has the same type of legs, with similar names. They are called: relationships, finances, physical health, mental health, social health, and spiritual health.

Naturally, the stronger each leg is, the better it will support your table of life. The great news is that if each leg is in place under your table and any one leg is damaged or kicked out from underneath, the other legs remaining in place will continue to support your table until the damaged leg is repaired. However, if one leg after another is damaged, kicked out, and neglected, the table will eventually fall.

Let's look at each leg in particular and learn how to ensure its strength and support under your table of life. Please note that entire books have been written on each one of these categories. My intention is to offer enough information for you to become aware of the importance of each leg, and then it's up to you.

## Relationships

The first leg under your life table is called relationships. This includes your immediate family, friends, and co-workers, as well as relationships held with bankers, drycleaners, mechanics, grocery store clerks, teachers, et cetera.

You can easily damage this leg by becoming too familiar with those close to you and sometimes losing respect for them all together. When this happens you may begin treating them like an old pair of shoes that is always in your closet—you know that they will always be there for you no matter how you treat them. This type of behavior usually shows up and begins to impact our most important relationships: our immediate family.

Husbands and wives should make a constant and conscientious effort to work towards a healthy relationship. Quality time alone should be planned on a weekly, if not daily, basis. If you don't plan for it and write it in your schedule, it most likely won't happen.

Remember the familiar pair of shoes? Sometimes my wife and I would finally get away from the kids (we dearly love our children), only to drive somewhere and sit in the parking lot and talk. Ah, time alone. Each planned time together does not have to be a major event, just as long as you are together and have each other's undivided attention.

Relationships should also be maintained and established between parents and their children. Dinnertime with the family has always been a priority in our family. Date nights are also special between you and your children, giving you that one-on-one time to focus on their concerns and interests. It is said that the average American family spend less than fifteen minutes per day together. That's tragic!

Unless a specific plan is made, time together never just seems to happen automatically. I've had many concerned parents ask me how they should go about developing a relationship with their "out of control" teenager. I always tell them that the relationship begins when the child is born.

Thinking that after some twelve years, a significant and deeply rooted relationship can be established in a short period of time is asking for a miracle. It is, however, never too late to start, but the later you begin the harder it will be. When significant time is spent with your children, significant relationships develop. Invest in your children early or pay the price later!

Friends should also have their time set aside. A great support network is vitally important in the life of anyone. Close friends will always provide an outlet for personal expression and sometimes much needed advice.

Managing your relationships with co-workers is very important as well. Much of your day will be spent with these people, so it is worth the effort to maintain good standing and integrity no matter what the cost. Who knows, one day you may be managing them or they may be managing you!

## Finance

The next leg under your table is called finance. This leg is usually the one that most people spend the greatest amount of time on, and with good reason. This should be a very strong leg because of the direct effect it has on everything else. However, if too much time is spent developing this leg, leaving the other legs weak, an unhealthy support structure will develop.

What good would all the money in the world be to someone who does not have the health or relationships to enjoy it with? The Beatle's were right when they used to sing, "can't buy me love." Money cannot buy you friends or health or anything of lasting value.

In fact, as you begin making more and more money, you will be surprised at what it attracts. It seems that money is a lure to those that don't have any. Don't get me wrong, having a lot of money is great, as long as it is in balance with everything else in your life. **You should always own money; it should never own you!**

Professional football player, Dion Sanders, once said, "Money has a tendency to make you more of what you already are." What a great truth!

If you have a tendency to gamble, more money would probably mean you would gamble more. If you have a tendency to buy expensive clothes, then guess what, more money will cause you to buy even more. Whatever your habits, more money will simply compound those habits. That's why it is vitally important to keep money and finance in balance with everything else in your life.

There are countless stories of people who have won the lottery one year only to be broke and/or divorced the next! Even the Bible states that money is not evil but the love of money is!

Making or receiving large amounts of money does not have to be a bad experience. I have had great luck in carefully studying and modeling other people who have had great long-term success with money and then adopted some of their behaviors to my own. There are many great books on money management and accounting available as well. The trick is to actually read and study good material from credible sources and then IMPLEMENT what you've learned for your own benefit.

This book is not a book on money management, but a few things should be reviewed as it relates to money and finance. Please answer the following: Have you set long and short term financial goals and written them down? Have you created a budget for your home and business that you consistently follow? Do you have adequate insurance and do you update at least once every year or as needed? Are your cash inflows greater than your outflows? How do you know? Do you have a good relationship with your accountant or CPA? Have you reviewed all of your credit card debt? Can you consolidate loans for better interest rates? Do you have enough equity in your home for an equity home loan that would pay all credit cards off and give you an interest write-off at the same time?

Are all your taxes paid up to date? Have you projected for next year? Any big expenditures forthcoming, like your children's college tuition, that you may need to begin saving for? Are you saving at least 10 percent of your income each month in a separate savings account for yourself? Are you tax planning for maximum write-offs? Are you giving a portion of your earnings to those in need?

The list could go on and on, but for the sake of time and space in this book, please note, the sooner you get started the better. Your goal should be to minimize all taxes and have your money working for you instead of you working for your money.

*Please note, because we usually receive more questions about finance than almost anything else, we now offer personal and business financial coaching—our contact information is located in the back of this book.*

Once you've spent quality time gathering good financial information and advice, then apply it to your individual set of circumstances and the leg of finance should stand strong under your table of life.

## Physical health

The next leg under your table pertains to your physical health. Are you in pretty good shape or could you be better? Advancements and studies in health and fitness are at all time highs. It is reported that more than four billion dollars is spent annually in the United States on weight loss products and services alone!

If you are not in good physical shape or do not have the energy you want, I encourage you to find help immediately—it's now more available than ever. Remember earlier when I asked, what good would all the money in the world be if you didn't have the health to enjoy it? If you don't want to improve your energy and health for yourself, do it for those who love you. You may read this and say, "I'm in pretty good shape," but if you aren't following a program that makes exercise and/or eating right a part of your everyday activity, then please take action now. You'll be so glad you did!

I operate at such a higher level of output when I'm in better shape. I also know I'll never have the physique of a body builder or be as lean as an endurance athlete, but there are things I can do on a daily basis to improve my health and increase my energy . . . and so can you!

The first step to take towards better health is to become aware of where you are now compared to where you want to be. If you haven't had a physical and blood work done recently, start with that. A consultation with your doctor will give you a greater understanding of your internal biophysical health and its role in how you look and feel. An accurate picture of where you are now will be important to reference as you begin to measure your progress. Remember, people will never do what you expect but will generally always do what you inspect, so inspect yourself!

Upon completion of your blood work and physical, talk to your doctor about your health goals and allow him or her to make recommendations based on where you are now. If you don't think you can make changes on your own, hire a trainer, a life coach, or enlist a partner who will commit to consistent exercise and healthy eating.

It has been my experience that if I haven't invested money in something, I don't give it very much credibility and wind up not "sticking with it." Therefore, if at all possible, invest in your health. Join a health club, buy healthy foods, buy books on exercise and fitness, or hire a trainer or a life coach. Just do something—invest in yourself!

Physical health is a very important leg under your table of life. If your health is in jeopardy, your entire life is affected.

## Mental health

The next leg under your table pertains to your mental health. What are you doing to keep an active mind? Are you learning anything new? Staying current with the latest relevant information? How much do you read? Is it making you a better person? If you watch television, what do you watch? Is it enriching your life? Is it entertainment only or do you balance it with educational programming? When is the last time you did a crossword puzzle or something that made you think? Have you taken a class lately?

It is vitally important to stay mentally sharp. Have you heard the old saying, "If you don't use it, you'll lose it"? That is so true in regards to your mind. Scientists say that our brain is like hundreds of supercomputers all running at once. Its full capacity is not even calculable.

Since the brain is arguably the most important part of our bodies, how are you taking care of yours? What are you doing to keep it sharp and clear? Try and stimulate your brain at least once a week with something new and challenging. After you create a habit of stimulation, then work on increasing frequency.

The great thing about stimulating your brain is that as you stimulate one area, other areas are stimulated as well. You may be doing a crossword puzzle or playing scrabble and wake up the next morning with a new idea because you are waking up places in your brain that haven't been exercised recently.

Now go exercise your brain and establish another leg under your table of life!

## Social health

The next leg under your table pertains to your social health. This is very closely tied to relationships and most of the same principals apply.

The most important element in your social health is to interact with people who support and lift you up. It is so hard to be around people with negative attitudes and poor dispositions. Since you know how important it is to monitor what you listen to and what you speak, it will be even more important to monitor the type of people you are around.

I'm not saying be a snob, but I am saying that if the people you associate with do not respect your request for positive comments and conversations, you should take a close look at finding more positive influences in your life, as this will be very important to your long-term success.

There will be occasions when you are the only one giving out support to the people around you and that's fine as along as you also have people who encourage you when needed. A car can only run so long before it needs to fill up with gas!

Social events should be attended in balance as well and may include special gatherings, parties, church activities, or voluntary activities. I've known some people who must attend EVERY social event no matter what! They live to be seen by others and will sacrifice anything to attend every event possible. There are even some who think attending social events is the only way to gain promotion or influence.

Again, all things done in balance, social events should be mixed into your life with the balance needed for long-term success. Once accomplished, this leg may be added under your table as well.

## Spiritual health

The next leg under your table pertains to your spiritual health. This topic alone could be discussed until the end of time and has many different angles and viewpoints. Therefore, I will share only what I have experienced personally and then suggest you decide what is best for you.

Growing up as a preacher's kid, I gained exposure to all sorts of activities that would fall under the umbrella of religion or spirituality. Yes, I bucked the system, tried to disprove everything that I had ever been taught, and was a genuine rebel!

After trying everything, the net result was that I didn't believe in religion, but absolutely entrusted everything in my life to a relationship with my Creator—a relationship rather than a religion.

I found that religion is man's attempt to communicate with God in a specific way. Many times these "ways" are built entirely on tradition and never questioned. In many religions if these "ways" are not followed to the letter, then severe consequences ensue—including total exclusion! If never questioned, negative belief systems may develop and overall spirituality is hindered.

In my studies of the Bible, it seems that the only people Jesus ever really got mad at were the religious leaders who seemed more concerned with their own laws and rules than the condition of their heart and how it related to their Creator and their fellow man.

Jesus, who is known as the Son of God, broke most of the religious leaders' rules, while at the same time performing great miracles—a genuine rebel! He was ultimately getting more results than any of them! This infuriated the religious leaders and they turned on Him. As I questioned my own faith and went on a quest to prove it wrong, I discovered these five primary truths:

1. There is a God who loves me for who I am, independent of my religious affiliations.

2. He sent His son to die for my sins and upon my acknowledgement of that fact (even if it is by faith, because I can't see it or fully understand

it), I am considered a child of God and have secured my eternal home.

3. Nothing can separate me from the love of my heavenly Father—ever!

4. Upon becoming a child of God, my entire life changed for the better—my relationships, finances, physical, mental, social, and spiritual health all improved.

5. It was a free gift. I can't earn it, I didn't buy it, nor can I return it.

I can now rest in the fact that there is a good plan for my life designed by the Creator of all things.

When I think of creation and of the precision needed in the galaxies to allow the universe to even exist, it blows my mind. Consider if the earth were positioned just a few more degrees away from the sun. We would all freeze. If it were positioned just a few degrees closer to the sun, we would all burn.

Look at how the vast oceans are kept in check and clean themselves by tides that are regulated by the moon. See how the plants and trees give off oxygen so that we may breathe and live, how everything works in exact precision. What an awesome God!

Upon my quest for spirituality, I came to acknowledge that saying there was no God was like saying Webster's dictionary was the result of an explosion in a print factory and all the words just fell into place on their own!

Even if I threw all logic aside and said it all just happened with a big bang, I still would want to know who pulled the trigger that made the "Big Bang"!

I thought to myself, "If people can have faith in something they have never seen, such as the "Big Bang" or origination by evolution, then I should have faith in a big God of whom people have seen on earth through the recorded accounts of Jesus Christ.

Jesus had such an impact on history that He split time in half. He is the reason we refer to time as B.C., (before Christ), and A.D., (after His death). The man who had such an impact on his followers (the ones who traveled with Him and saw the miracles He performed) that even when He was gone, they were willingly killed, stoned, boiled in hot oil, filleted alive, and beheaded, rather than deny His existence.

What an impression! How intense must their relationship have been with Jesus to endure such grueling deaths rather than deny His existence?

If people can have faith in slime that just happened to come together and form the right way, crawl out from a pond and turn into an intelligent human being, then I can have faith in a loving heavenly father who created me as the object of His affections and pre-designed me for success in all areas of my life. And then, even with all that power, didn't demand that I do anything, but gave me a choice to accept it.

This Creator left me an instruction manual for life called the Bible. The most widely read book in the world and on best sellers lists for over two thousand years! Over five thousand specific prophecies are recorded in the Bible, of which over four thousand have already came true exactly how they were prophesied thousands of years earlier!

Again, this is my belief and the example I choose to follow. I will never talk about religion, but I **must** talk about a relationship that I have with my Creator that has literally changed every area of my life for the better! I guess you could say it has strengthened all the other legs under my table of life.

So, if each leg under your table is developed and secure in place, your table of life will stand no matter what. Even if one or two legs get weak or even kicked out from underneath, with all the legs in place under your table, you'll still be able to stand strong while the damaged legs are being repaired.

# ❧ Now It Is Your Turn ❧

Make a list of all six legs under your table of life, in your journal. Next to each leg, list at least five things you can do to strengthen and secure that leg.

Commit now to the implementation of at least one action per week until each leg is STRONG. Remember to write down your goals in strengthening your legs so that you can measure your progress and see results.

Modeling other successful people in each of these areas would be a great first step, but it is up to you to actually do this. You owe it to yourself and to the ones you love.

# Chapter Eleven

# Leaving a Legacy
## —Lasting Impressions

$\mathcal{W}$hat is legacy? Merriam-Webster's dictionary says: a legacy is "something transmitted by or received from an ancestor or predecessor or from the past." In essence, legacy is what you will be known for as well as what you will have handed down to the next generation.

Your legacy will have an immediate impact on your children and grandchildren, but will also have an impact on others within your circle of influence.

Leaving a legacy is much more than money, property, homes, cars, et cetera. Material goods are definitely a part of legacy, but not the only part. Some of the more significant things that you will be handing down as part of your legacy include traits such as, your attitude, work ethic, family traditions, and the overall way you live your life.

## Within your immediate family

You have probably heard that a picture is worth a thousands words? What people see you do, especially

your immediate family, is what impacts them the most.
For example:

☐ How do you treat your family on a daily basis?

☐ Is it customary for you to yell, scream, and throw things in your house?

☐ When answering the phone, if you don't want to talk, do you ask others to lie for you and say your not there?

☐ If you don't feel like going to work, do you ever call in sick when you truthfully are not?

☐ Do you pay your bills on time or have you taught your family how to sidestep bill collectors?

☐ When you start something, do you always finish it?

☐ Are you on time?

☐ Do you do what you say when you said you would do it?

☐ Does your house stay clean?

☐ Is your car clean and tags up to date?

☐ Is the yard kept nice?

☐ Do you talk about other people behind their backs?

☐ Do you gossip?

❏ Do you attend church?

❏ Are you faithful in your relationships?

Okay, I'll stop, but please note that each of these traits—each way you act in front of your immediate family, will ultimately serve as a trait handed down as part of your legacy. Do you want your children and grandchildren to act the way you act right now, in every area of your life, for generations to come? If not, as long as you have breathe, there is time to change and improve.

## With those you influence

Let's look at how legacy will impact those outside of your immediate family. It says in the Bible that a good name is more precious than gold—how true! Your reputation will follow you and your family for years to come.

I may have relatives in my extended family that have not made good choices in life. Because of that, if anyone hears my last name and can link it to one of them, my reputation is immediately called into question.

This is one of the primary reasons that particular ethnic groups have been labeled and treated certain ways—because of their legacy. When the majority of a particular ethnic group act a certain way, over a certain period of time a reputation is formed and it is not long before everyone in that group is treated the same way.

The same goes for religious groups and clubs. How would you feel if you were suddenly surrounded by a group of Hell's Angels? Why would you feel that way? I'm sure there may be good individuals in that particular group, but their reputation as a group precedes them. Therefore, you would treat everyone in the group the same.

The pitt bull has certain tenacious qualities, as we have discussed, but for those same reasons, if I pass a pitt bull on a jogging trail that isn't on a leash, I immediately begin to treat it based on its legacy. It might be the most gentle, docile dog in the park, but based on its reputation, I have a predetermined way of reacting to its presence. It was bred to be a fighting dog . . . what more do I need to know!

## Dr. Martin Luther King

Dr. Martin Luther King Jr. is one of the greatest examples in history of a man who was determined to change and enhance his legacy for himself, his family, and his people. The changes he effected in his legacy even brought change in an entire country of people from all racial backgrounds.

King's grandfather began the family's long pastoral tenure at the Ebenezer Baptist Church in Atlanta, serving from 1914 to 1931. King's father then served until 1960, and until his death, King acted as co-pastor. That's a legacy right there!

King received his B.A. degree in 1948 from Morehouse College followed by three years of theological study at Crozer Theological Seminary in Pennsylvania. It was there he was elected president of a predominantly white senior class and was awarded the B.D. in 1951. He enrolled in Boston University and received his doctorate in 1955. It was in Boston that he met and married Coretta Scott, a young woman of uncommon intellectual and artistic attainments. Together, the Kings had two sons and two daughters.

In 1954, King accepted the pastorate of the Dexter Avenue Baptist Church in Montgomery, Alabama. King was always a strong worker for civil rights for the African-American race. He became a member of the executive committee of the National Association for the Advancement of Colored People, the leading organization of its kind in the nation. By the December of 1955, he accepted the leadership of the first great Negro nonviolent demonstration of contemporary times in the United States: the bus boycott.

The boycott lasted 382 days. On December 21, 1956, after the Supreme Court of the United States declared unconstitutional the laws requiring segregation on buses, blacks and whites rode the buses as equals. During the days of the boycott, King was arrested, his home was bombed, and he was subjected to personal abuse. King emerged as a leader, serving as an example of unity to a nation of onlookers.

In 1957 he was elected president of the Southern Christian Leadership Conference, an organization formed to provide new leadership for the now-burgeoning civil rights movement. The ideals for this organization were sourced from Christianity, and its operational techniques from Gandhi.

Between 1957 and 1968, King traveled over six million miles and spoke over 2,500 times, appearing wherever there was injustice, protest, and racial disharmony. He wrote five books and numerous articles. When he led the massive protest in Birmingham, Alabama that caught the attention of the entire world, it provided what he called a "coalition of conscience." When he was arrested from the demonstration, he wrote the powerful manifesto, *Letters from a Birmingham Jail.*

He directed the peaceful march of 250,000 in Washington D.C. where he delivered his address, "I Have a Dream." King conferred with President John F. Kennedy and campaigned for President Lyndon B. Johnson. He was arrested upwards of twenty times and assaulted at least four times. King was also awarded five honorary degrees, was named Man of the Year by *Time* magazine in 1963, and became not only the symbolic leader of American blacks but also a world figure of peace.

At the age of thirty-five, Martin Luther King Jr., was the youngest man to have received the Nobel Peace Prize. When notified of his selection, he announced that he would turn over the prize money of $54,123 to further the civil rights movement.

On the evening of April 4, 1968, while standing on the balcony of his motel room in Memphis, Tennessee, where he was to lead a protest march in sympathy with striking garbage workers of that city, he was assassinated.

"The ultimate measure of a man is not where he stands in moments of comfort and convenience, but where he stands at times of challenge and controversy," said King.

This is one of the greatest examples to date of a man who was determined to change and enhance the legacy he left for his family, his community, and his world.

**If you're unhappy with how people or society as a whole reacts to your family, gender, race, socioeconomic background, or anything else that helps form your identity, then it is up to you to change. Day after day, action after action, response after response, YOU will determine your legacy!**

If you are happy with your current identity, then it would be wise to make a special effort to teach your children, immediate family, and your circle of influence how to improve and continue that same legacy.

# ൕ  NOW IT IS YOUR TURN  ൖ

First, write down the behaviors in your life that you would like to continue and transfer to the "next generation", as part of your legacy. Also, include how and when you will teach those behaviors to your immediate family and circles of influence. Just by making those around you aware of the importance you've place on these behaviors is a great start. Remember, a picture is worth a thousand words, so continue to lead by example.

Next, write down the behaviors in your life that you do not want to transfer to the "next generation", as part of your legacy. Take the time now and write down how and when you will change those unwanted behaviors first, as you lead by example. Then, list how and when you will notify each of your family members and circles of influence of the importance you've placed on making those changes. Remember to model others and measure your own progress. Try to make at least one small change each day as you begin to form your new legacy. Your family, friends and circles of influence will be so grateful you did—for "generations" to come!

WOW! You've unwrapped your gift, revealed it to the world, learned how to implement it, learned how to measure its progress, learned how to live it in balance and how to leave it to your friends, family, and circles of influence! How does it feel to be ranked in the upper 1 percent of the population? You did it!

You are now armed and dangerous! Never again will you stand for mediocrity or shrink back from opportunity. You will become ALL you were born to be!

Congratulations and God bless!

# Contact Information

Henry A. Penix

P.O. Box 8010

Tulsa, OK 74101-8010

Telephone: 918.447.8880

Fax: 918.447.8881

Web sites:

www.hapm.com

www.ayd.info

# About the Author

Henry A. Penix is speaking into the hearts and lives of today's generation, all around the world. He is a father of three and resides with his wife and family in Tulsa, OK.

Growing a company successfully from two employees to more than three hundred, Mr. Penix, now financially independent, has dedicated his life to teaching others how they too can do the same.

Starting without enough money to buy his own weddings rings ($130 dollars), a life of pain, chaos, and confusion was turned into a life of health, peace, and eternal perspective.

His book, *Accelerate Your Destiny*, was recently on Amazon.com's top ten list and has been translated into Spanish and German. Mr. Penix will complete his much anticipated European tour this year.

Living life at its lowest and being blessed into abundance, Mr. Penix communicates experientially, not from a book that he's read but from a life that he's led, into the hearts and lives of each person looking to improve in any area of their life. He has been awarded with the following achievements:

- Recipient of SBA's Entrepreneur of the Year Award

- Recipient of the Blue Chip Enterprise Initiative Award

- Received commendations from Governor Walters, as well as the Senate and House of Representatives, for leadership

- Recipient of Honorary Doctorate Degree of Christian Leadership

## What others are saying about Accelerate Your Destiny (AYD) Business & Life Coaching . . .

### Iowa – Life-coaching client
I've read most of Steven Covey's work. I have Anthony Robbins' audio and books, Norman Vincent Peale, Brian Tracy, and the list goes on. I teach people in corporations how to identify their goals, create a plan and accomplish their objectives. I really wasn't sure that my *Accelerate Your Destiny* life coach, or anyone else, could give me anything new. However, I did know that I needed help for life to be as I felt it should be. Thank you for coaching and facilitating my journey. I now feel I'm on the right path to do great things.

### New York – Life-coaching & business-coaching client
With the AYD principles I started my own company and doubled my income thanks to your explosive message and the powerful step-by-step system.

### Las Vegas - Life-coaching client
Before I enrolled in *Accelerate Your Destiny,* I was wanting to increase the profitability of my business, but I needed to learn the principles necessary to achieve the results I wanted. After AYD, I made some critical changes to my business and am heading in a new direction that will help me achieve my financial goals as well as live a life of happiness and peace that I didn't know I could have. I am thankful that your program covers all aspects of life!

### North Carolina – Business-coaching client
I have increased my business 46 percent in the past sixty days since beginning your coaching program.

<u>_Washington_</u> – *Life-coaching client*
Words cannot express my gratefulness to you and your program. You've allowed me to become aware of many personal belief systems that were holding me back. I can't wait to utilize the group coaching.

<u>_North Carolina_</u> - *Business-coaching client*
I was able to identify some patterns in my sales that have allowed me to make some changes that will yield great financial return!

<u>_Oklahoma_</u> – *Life-coaching client & business-coaching client*
Accelerate Your Destiny has given me the tools necessary to balance my life. Now my priorities and finances are in line, and I even have time to do things for myself.

<u>_Wisconsin_</u> - *Business-coaching client*
Through AYD, I have been shown a new way of looking at my circumstances, particularly relating to my business, and have been able to recognize and implement new systems and processes that have allowed me to streamline my efforts.

<u>_Texas_</u> – *Life-coaching client*
The AYD coaching staff is made up of the most top-notch people in their field. They aren't afraid to ask the difficult questions and help you discover the answers. Don't be concerned about the investment: these people are genuinely concerned about your growth. They are there because they have a burning desire and vision to help those who want to earnestly discover their destinies.

<u>_North Carolina_</u> - *Business-coaching client*
While participating in AYD, I experienced huge break-throughs both personally and in my business. I was able to break through a self-limiting belief that has always stifled my personal and professional development.

*Georgia* - *Business-coaching client*
I was able to recognize the need for better organization in my business and implement the awesome techniques I learned in the program. It has made a difference in my productivity and increased my focus!

*North Carolina* - *Business-coaching client*
I have dramatically improved my time management skills by implementing strategies I learned in the AYD program. Now, I am able to accomplish twice as many calls daily which drastically increases my sales.

*North Carolina* - *Business-coaching client*
Through the AYD Business Coaching Program, I have recognized the importance of planning my day, prioritizing and setting time frames for task completion. Now I'm able to complete what needs to be done each day and I'm more aware of when I become distracted or diverted.

*Texas* - *Business-coaching client*
I've learned how to delegate and train others so that my message gets out faster—working smarter and not harder.

*North Carolina* - *Business-coaching client*
I'm now using information I had learned before but didn't use. This program, particularly the accountability, moved me to action. Knowledge is not the problem—it's applied knowledge. AYD moved me to action and helped ensure that I was applying my knowledge.

*North Carolina* - *Business-coaching client*
The program was a great way for group members to be a help and resource to one another. The group dynamics brought solutions that I had never thought of.

# Accelerate Your Destiny
# Life & Business Coaching

Congratulations! Now that you have unwrapped your gift, allow Accelerate Your Destiny (AYD) to help coach you through its complete implementation.

- Our professional coaching staff will use their combined knowledge and resources, accumulated over several years, to help accelerate your success as you avoid the pitfalls others experience only through trial and error.

- Learn the same tips, tools, and techniques proven successful from clients all over the world.

- Personal or Business, AYD has a specific plan for you.

For additional information, contact our coaching staff at 1.800.260.4603 or look at our Web site at www.AYD.info.